MYTHOLOGY

A COOPERATIVE LEARNING UNIT

PRESTWICK HOUSE, INC.

"Everything for the English Classroom!"

Prestwick House, Inc.
P.O. Box 658
Clayton, Delaware 19938

Editor: Dr. James Scott
Associate Editor: Paul Moliken
Design: Larry Knox
Production: Jerry Clark
Manufacturing: Victor Graphics

ISBN 978-1-58049-106-8

About The Cover Picture

While the Cyclops, Polyphemus, is best known as one of Odysseys' main adversaries, our
cover picture refers to a different incident in Polyphemus' life. The painting, done by a student of Raphael, Giulio Pippi (1492 – 1546), depicts a love-struck Polyphemus attempting to
woo the beautiful Galatea. Galatea, seated on the edge of a cliff with her sister, however, is
not won over by the songs of love that Polyphemus has played and sung to her.

CONTENTS

PRONUNCIATION GUIDE

Achilles - (uh KIL eez)
Acrisius - (uh KREE see uhs)
Aegisthus - (uh GIS thus)
Aeschylus - (ES kuh luhs)
Aeneas - (uh NEE uhs)
Agamemnon - (ag uh MEM non)
Andromeda - (an DROM e da)
Antigone - (an TIG uh nee)
Aphrodite - (af ruh DIE tee)
Arachne - (uh RAK nee)
Ares - (AIR-eez)
Argonauts (AHR guh nauts)
Ariadne - (uh REE ad nae)
Artemis - (AHR tuh muhs)
Augean - (aw JEE uhn)
Aurora - (aw ROAR uh)
Baucis - (BAW kiss)
Bacchus - (BAHK us)
Boreas - (BOHR ee us)
Cecrops - (SEE krahps)
Cephalus - (SEF uh lus)
Cepheus - (see FEE us)
Cerberus - (SUR buh ruhs)
Ceres - (SEER eez)
Charon - (KAIR uhn)
Charybdis - (kuh RIB dis)
Circe - (SUR see)
Clytemnestra - (cly tem NES tra)
Clytie - (KLY tee)
Creüsa - (KREE suh)
Cyclops - (sy KLOPS)
Daedalus - (ded L uhs)
Danaïds - (Di NAY i deez)
Diomedes - (die AH mi deez)
Dionysus - (die uh NEE suhs)
Dryope - (dry O pay)

Eetes - (EE teez)
Eurystheus - (u RIS thee uhs)
Epimetheus - (ep i MEE thee uhs)
Glaucus - (GLAW kus)
Hades - (HAY deez)
Helios - (HE lee ohs)
Hephaestus - (he FES tuhs)
Hermes - (HER meez)
Icarus - (IK uh ruhs)
Io - (EYE o)
Ion - (EYE own)
Iphigenia - (if uh juh NI uh)
Medea - (mi DEE uh)
Narcissus - (nar SIS uhs)
Oedipus - (ED uh puhs)
Orestes - (aw RES teez)
Orithyia - (o RITH ee uh)
Pelias - (pe LE uhs)
Perseus - (PER see uhs)
Philomela - (fil o MEE luh)
Philemon - (FILL e mon)
Phineus - (FIN ee uhs)
Pomona - (po MO nuh)
Procne - (PROK nee)
Procris - (PRO kris)
Procrustes - (pro KRUS teez)
Prometheus - (pro MEE thee uhs)
Proserpine - (PROS ur peen)
Psyche - (SI kee)
Pygmalion - (pig MAY lee uhn)
Pyramus - (PEER a mus)
Scylla - (SIL uh)
Theseus - (THEE see uhs)
Thisbe - (THIS bee)
Tiresias - (tie REE see uhs)
Zephyr - (ZEF uhr)

CHAPTER 1

THE BEGINNING OF THE WORLD –
AS THE GREEKS SAW IT

In the Beginning

IN THE BEGINNING, there was nothing but blackness, but slowly out of the blackness stepped Mother Earth. It was she who created Cronus and his wife Rhea to be rulers of the earth, and it was she who warned Cronus that one day one of his sons would murder him and take over his rule.

Cronus sat down and scratched his head. He was very troubled, for it happened that he and his wife were expecting their first babies any day now. Suddenly, a simple and practical answer came to him. Standing up, he said, "I will defeat the prophecy by swallowing each baby as soon as it is born." True to his word, Cronus devoured five of his children the minute each was born. Furious, Rhea swore to herself that Cronus would not do the same to her sixth child. When she was ready to deliver Zeus, her sixth baby, Rhea went off by herself. After giving birth to Zeus, she hid him in a tree. Then she picked up a large rock, wrapped it in a baby blanket and, holding it to her breast, walked home.

Seeing her, Cronus demanded, "What do you have in the blanket?"

"Only a stone," said Rhea.

"I'll bet," he said. "Pull the blanket away."

"No," Rhea replied.

"It's a baby and I'm going to swallow it just as I did the other five." With this, Cronus snatched the bundle from Rhea's arms. Stuffing it into his mouth, he swallowed it as if it were a large vitamin pill.

The next day, a very sick Cronus threw up the stone and each of his five swallowed children one by one. When these five grew up, they aided Zeus in his battle against Cronus.

In addition to his brothers and sisters, Zeus had some powerful monsters on his side. The Cyclopes were mammoth beasts with one eye in the center of their foreheads. The Hundred-Handed Ones had fifty heads apiece and hated Cronus for having imprisoned them in the underworld.

On Cronus' side was a race of giants called Titans, and the strongest and mightiest of these was Atlas. After Zeus and his allies defeated Cronus, Zeus pondered over a fitting punishment for Atlas.

"Kill him," said Zeus' brother Hades.

"Yes, drown him," said Poseidon.

"No," said Zeus. "Let's punish him with a task. We'll make him spend eternity carrying the heavens on his shoulders."

You can still see Atlas on the covers of certain maps, kneeling on one knee with the world on his shoulders.

The brothers now turned their attention to their newly-won domains and the question of which of them should rule over what. After much arguing, they decided to toss dice to determine the answer. Zeus won the first toss and chose to be rule the heavens. This choice pleased Poseidon, who chose to be ruler of the oceans, and it left Hades with two choices. Hades, who could elect to be ruler of the earth or of the underworld, chose the underworld. ❂

Zeus and Family

TIME PASSED AND Zeus decided he wanted a wife. His mother, Rhea, was indignant.

"You marry? Don't be crazy! You spend all your time chasing women. You could never be faithful to one. I forbid it. You would be unhappy, your wife would be unhappy, and all creatures in the heavens and on the earth would be made unhappy."

"You *forbid* it?" sneered Zeus. "I am the master of the heavens! I'll do what I want."

"No, you won't! You'll do as I say," replied Rhea. "I'm sick of it. You're always changing into some animal or other to pursue some pretty mortal."

When Zeus defied her and married his sister Hera, Rhea never said a word. She had been right, though, for Zeus continued to chase women and Hera was murderously jealous. As a result, the two were constantly at war.

Sometimes innocent mortal girls got involved with Zeus without knowing his true identity. Zeus slyly visited earth in the form of a beautiful animal. Once he had drawn a girl's attention in this disguise, he would work his magic on her. The poor girl was helpless to resist.

Despite Zeus' wandering eye, Hera soon had three children by him. Their first son, Ares, became the god of war. The Romans called him "Mars."

Their second son, Hephaestus, was the god of the forge and patron of all craftsmen. Their daughter Eris took great pleasure riding in her brother Ares' chariot. As she rode, Eris would scream and howl in such a fashion that she struck fear into the hearts of all mortals who heard her. For this, Eris became known as the goddess of discord.

Zeus also had a number of illegitimate children by other women. One of the most well-known of these children was Athena. Her mother, a Titan goddess, had changed into a fish, a bird, and a snake in order to get away from Zeus, but in the end he caught her. At first, Zeus was pleased when the Titan goddess became pregnant, but then he was told the following prophecy:

"While the first child will be a girl, beware of the second child. For if a male child is born of your union, he will do to you what you did to Cronus."

Like his father, Zeus decided to try to play it safe. He swallowed both the Titan goddess and her unborn female baby. Within an hour, though, Zeus got a headache so intolerable that he ran to his son Hephaestus and begged him to split open his head.

Zeus lay his head on Hephaestus' anvil, and Hephaestus reluctantly split it open for him. Now the cause of Zeus' headache was visible. A tall young woman in a full suit of armor sprang fully-grown from Zeus' head. Zeus named her Athena and made her the goddess of wisdom. Athena was so popular with the ancient Greeks that they named Athens, a major city, after her.

Another of Zeus' illegitimate children was Apollo, who is often shown driving his chariot across the heavens, pulling the sun behind it. For this reason, Apollo is sometimes called the sun god, but he was also the god of light, science, and the arts. Apollo established the Oracle at Delphi, a temple in which people sought answers from the gods and predictions about the future. The gods spoke to the mortals through a priest. Because the wording of the priest's answers could be taken in different ways, the priest's answers could never be wrong—though they might be tricky. When one emperor asked the Oracle at Delphi if he should make war on Persia, he was told that a great empire would be overthrown if he did. He did make war and an empire was overthrown, but the empire was his own.

Another goddess who was sometimes said to be a daughter of Zeus was Aphrodite, the goddess of love and beauty. Other stories claim she was born from the foam of the sea. When Zeus saw Aphrodite, he thought she was the most beautiful being he had ever seen and took her immediately to Mount Olympus. When they arrived, Hera took one look at Aphrodite and said, "This girl will be nothing but trouble. The gods will kill each other over the chance to win her hand. Get her married at once."

Zeus brushed off Hera's warning, but Hera proved right. All of the gods were captivated by Aphrodite's beauty, and all wanted her for their own. To end the fighting, Zeus quickly married her off to his son Hephaestus. Hephaestus was not a handsome god and had lost the use of his legs when he was thrown as a child from Mount Olympus by an angry Zeus (or, some say, Hera). Since Zeus decreed that she had to marry someone, though, Aphrodite thought it might as well be Hephaestus. She knew that the beautiful jewelry her husband would craft for her would further set off her own beauty, and she relished the idea of a husband who was too slow to chase her. Hephaestus' inability to walk, thought Aphrodite, would enable her to sneak off and have affairs with other gods. The Greeks knew that there were two sides to love and beauty: one good and one devious and potentially harmful.

Another dual-natured god was Dionysus. The son of Zeus and a mortal, Dionysus was the god of wine and revelry, and it was he who taught humans how to turn the juice of

Hermes, another of Zeus' illegitimate sons, also displayed two natures. Usually portrayed as an attractive, graceful youth, Hermes is best known as the messenger of the gods and a guardian of travelers. As a child, however, Hermes was a mischievous trickster and thief, so he is also the patron god of thieves and rascals. In ancient art, Hermes is depicted in a hat with wings and winged sandals, carrying a staff that has a snake twined about it. You may recognize Hermes by his Roman name, Mercury. ❂

Hera, Zeus, and Io

ONE AFTERNOON AS Hera was lounging in the sun on Mount Olympus, the world suddenly grew dark. Hera was immediately suspicious that Zeus had created this darkness to hide the fact that he was with another woman. She stood up and started to call for Zeus. Hearing no answer, she brushed away some of the clouds at her feet and peered down at the earth. Zeus was there, standing on the bank of a river next to an astonishingly beautiful young calf. Knowing Zeus' old trick of disguising himself or his love interests as animals, Hera decided to drop down and investigate.

While Hera was sometimes overly suspicious, this time she was right. Zeus had been flirting with Io, the daughter of a river god. On hearing Hera call, he quickly turned to Io and said, " I'm going to turn you into a calf. Don't be frightened."

Io couldn't help being frightened, and, her voice shaking, asked, "Why?"

the grape into wine. The Romans called Dionysus "Bacchus" and celebrated him with wild, excessive, and seemingly endless parties. Today such parties are sometimes called "bacchanalias."

The Greeks recognized the fact that alcohol could be both a blessing and a curse. This is evident in tales of a group of women called the Maendes. Followers of Dionysus, the Maendes lived in the forest and were usually harmless. Whenever they drank too much wine, though, these women became vicious killers, tearing innocent people limb from limb.

"Because," Zeus answered, "if Hera finds us together, she'll bother me and make things unpleasant for you."

"But we haven't done anything," protested Io.

"That won't make any difference to Hera," Zeus said. "She'll punish you just because I looked at you." With this, Zeus turned Io into a calf and she lost the ability to protest any further. Hera arrived his side almost immediately. "What are you up to?" she demanded.

"I just came to visit the river," he replied.

"I see," she said. Pointing at the calf, she asked, "What is this beauty and to whom does it belong?"

"That?" said Zeus casually. "That is a calf. It was given to me by a river god, but I have no use for it. I'm going to chase it off."

"Don't do that," Hera said slyly. "If you don't want the calf, I'll take it."

Now Zeus was in a difficult position. He didn't want to give Io to his wife, but any objection would further fan the flames of Hera's suspicion. Finally, with a shrug, he said, "Do as you like."

Hera was not fooled by Zeus' casual manner. She took the calf to a hundred-eyed man she knew named Argus.

"Argus," she ordered, "Keep a strict watch over this creature."

His one hundred eyes made Argus an ideal guard. Even when he slept he never closed more than two eyes at a time, keeping the other ninety-eight fixed on his prisoner. During the day, Argus let Io graze and roam freely, but at night he tied a rope around her neck and kept her tied to a nearby post.

Io, who would have begged Argus for her freedom if she had arms to stretch out or a voice to speak, became sadder and sadder. Her heart broke one day when she saw her father and sister walking through a field. Running after them, she tried to cry "Father!" but she could not form the words. Io trotted beside the pair, bleating desperately. At this, her father turned and said, "What a pretty calf. Come, let me pet your head." He knelt and stroked Io's head, admiring her beauty. Pulling up some grass, he held it out for her to eat, and she licked his hand.

"How," she cried to herself, "can I let him know who I am? If only I could speak my name."

Rising, her father said, "Good-bye, little calf. I must continue the search for my daughter."

Io became very excited. She tried to grab the bottom of her father's garment in her mouth to keep him from leaving, but, determined to resume his search, her father walked on.

Suddenly, a thought came to Io. Racing after her family, she caught up to them in a sandy area by the river. Panting, Io traced her name in the sand with her foot. Her father immediately recognized the large *I* and *O* and understood the significance of the message. Bending down, he embraced the calf by its neck and moaned, "Alas, my daughter, what crime could you have committed to deserve this? What god did you offend? It would be easier to see you dead than to see you captured in so unnatural a form."

While Io's father was speaking, Argus had drawn close.

"Enough of this crying and screaming," Argus said. "You'll upset the calf." Argus drove Io back to his post while her wretched father looked on helplessly.

Zeus, who had watched this scene, was troubled over Io's undeserved suffering. Determined to end it, he called Hermes to his side.

"Hermes, free that calf from the clutches of Argus," Zeus said.

Frowning, Hermes replied, "Father, I've lost every battle that I have ever had with Argus. I shall try, but I do not know if I can beat him."

"Beat him with your wits, not your might," said Zeus. "Use your trickery to put him to sleep; then cut off his head."

Pulling on his winged sandals and clutching his magical flute, Hermes leapt from the heavens to the earth below.

As Hermes made his way toward Argus, he put aside his winged sandals and cap and took on the appearance of a simple shepherd boy. He gathered a few sheep that were grazing on a hill and walked behind them, playing a beautiful tune on his flute. Hearing it,

Argus smiled with delight and called to Hermes.

"Young man, come and sit by me on this rock. You will not find a better or more pleasant place to graze your sheep."

"I can't," Hermes said coyly, "for my master may get mad."

"Of course you can. If your master complains, send him to me. I'll take care of him." Holding out the jug of wine he had at his side, Argus said, "Here, take a drink of my wine."

"Thank you, kind sir," Hermes said, "and for your kindness, allow me to play you some songs."

Hermes played lullaby after lullaby all afternoon, hoping to induce Argus to close each of his one hundred eyes. The task began to seem impossible, for, while many of his eyes did close, Argus always kept a few of them open.

Late in the day, Hermes began a story about some water nymphs. Whether because of the late hour or the length of the tale, this story did its work. Every one of Argus' one hundred eyes closed. As the watchman's head nodded forward, Hermes quietly drew his sword and slashed through Argus' neck with one quick stroke. Argus head tumbled down on the rocks, and all one hundred of his eyes fell out and rolled all over the ground.

Yawning and stretching, Hermes was preparing to whisk Io away when he caught sight of an outraged Hera coming towards him. Fearing her wrath, Hermes dropped Io and vanished from the spot.

Hera took in the scene immediately. She saw Hermes disappear, the calf taking off over a hill, and Argus' bloody head on the ground. As she stood there, a plain-looking peacock with a huge tail walked by. To honor her dead guard, Hera deposited Argus' one hundred eyes on the tail of the peacock, where they still may be seen to this day.

Hera was livid at Zeus and Hermes, but Zeus was too powerful and Hermes too quick for her to punish. Instead, Hera wreaked her revenge on Io. Snapping her fingers, she produced a huge fly with wicked teeth.

"Gadfly," she said, "catch up with and torment that calf. Sting it, bite it, and chase it all over the world. Let it not get a moment's rest."

Thus began Io's miserable journey. The gadfly chased Io over the plains, into the mountains, and across the seas. Today, anyone who repeatedly stings or verbally hounds another is still called a gadfly.

Zeus finally did come to Io's aid. He convinced Hera to end her torment and return Io to human form. In return, he agreed not to pay any further attention to Io. Gradually, Io's horns shrank and the coarse hair fell in clumps from her body until there was nothing left of the calf about her. It was as the beautiful girl that she had been that Io returned to her waiting family. ❖

Prometheus and Pandora

PROMETHEUS, WHOSE NAME means "forethought," was a Titan of great courage. Unlike most of the Titans, Prometheus had sided with Zeus in Zeus' battle with Cronus. At the time, Prometheus thought

that Zeus would make the world a better place for humans.

Soon Prometheus saw that Zeus did not aim to help the mortals. Instead, to keep people in their place and from trying to take his, Zeus sent them terrible suffering. At one point, Zeus ordered Poseidon to raise a flood that destroyed nearly everyone on earth. It was his aim to get the respect from them that he thought he deserved.

Zeus' tyrannical acts ate at Prometheus, and Prometheus began to look for a way to assist the defenseless humans. At the time, fire did not exist on earth, and its use was only permitted to the gods in the heavens. Prometheus decided to steal fire from the gods and give it to the mortals.

One evening on Mount Olympus, Prometheus stole to the hearth and lit some underbrush. Hiding the fire in a bowl, he brought it down to earth.

"You can now use heat to forge tools and weapons," he told the mortals. "With these, you can build better homes and farms, kill and roast animals for food, protect your families, and improve your lives."

When Zeus discovered the theft, he vowed to punish Prometheus. First, though, he wanted to make the mortals suffer. He decided to solicit the help of Hephaestus in this plan.

"Hephaestus," he said. "Using Aphrodite as a model, sculpt me the most beautiful and irresistible of women. Because she will possess all gifts, we shall call her Pandora."

When Hephaestus finished, Zeus breathed the spirit of life into Pandora, set her on earth, and commanded her to find

Prometheus and offer herself as his wife. Before she left, Zeus placed the germ of curiosity into Pandora and handed her a mysterious sealed box. It was a gift for Prometheus, he said, and she was forbidden from opening it herself.

When Pandora tracked down and appeared before Prometheus, the Titan—sensing that there was something dangerous about the box and marriage offer—ordered her from his presence. His brother Epimetheus, however, fell in love with Pandora at first sight. Soon after, Epimetheus and Pandora were wed.

In their house sat the unopened box. Pandora was hopelessly drawn to it and desperate to find out what was inside. Finally—as Zeus had planned all along—her curiosity got the better of her. Pandora opened the box.

With a forceful blast, evil spirits shot out of the box and were let loose into the world. Anger, envy, misery, horror, pain—the list of ills that the Pandora unwittingly unleashed on mortals is almost endless. Struggling with the terrible box, Pandora finally managed to close it. By that time the only thing left in the box was "hope."

Now Zeus turned his wrath on Prometheus. Zeus ordered two powerful giants to carry Prometheus off to the Caucasus mountains. Once there, they chained Prometheus to a cliff and left him for the vultures that arrived every day at dawn. From dawn till nightfall, the huge, ravenous birds ate away at Prometheus' liver. During the night, Prometheus' liver grew back, only to be eaten again the next morning. Prometheus bore this torture for the rest of eternity. ❀

Comprehension Check

1. What does the word "gadfly" mean and what is its origin?

2. What was Zeus' chief fault? What power did he possess that he demonstrated on a number of occasions?

3. Over what domain were the following gods and goddesses associated?

   Hermes -

   Aphrodite -

   Athena -

   Hephaestus -

   Poseidon -

4. For what reason did Zeus punish Prometheus, and what was the punishment?

CHAPTER 2

HEROES AND MONSTERS

Hercules: The Greatest Hero of All

THIS TALE INVOLVES two of the most powerful figures in Greek Mythology, Atlas and Hercules, and concerns the eleventh of the Twelve Labors of Hercules. King Eurystheus of Thebes demanded that Hercules bring him several golden apples from the sacred garden of Hesperides. A vicious dragon guarded the apple tree and prevented anyone from entering the garden. On learning this, Hercules decided to try to flatter Atlas into helping him.

"Great and mighty Atlas, I have a problem I cannot solve without your generous help. You know a secret route into the garden of Hesperides. Could you get me some apples from the tree?"

"I would help you if I could," said Atlas, gesturing upwards. "But there is nobody with whom I can leave my burden."

It was Atlas' job to support the weight of the sky upon his shoulders, and in Hercules' request he saw an opportunity to rid himself of this tiresome task.

"I'll shoulder your burden for you while you go," said Hercules. "Just transfer the weight of the sky to my back, and I'll hold it up while you go after the apples."

Atlas shifted the burden from his back to Hercules', lumbered off, and was back in a short time with the rare golden apples. To the surprise and frustration of Hercules, Atlas refused to reshoulder his burden.

"O, no—I've held up the sky long enough. You're strong enough; you do it from now on."

Quickly recovering his wits, Hercules groaned and said, "Oh, the pain of this load. If only I could ease it a bit. Atlas, would you mind taking the weight just long enough for me to place my lion's skin on my back so it won't chafe?" Foolishly, Atlas agreed, and Hercules grabbed the golden apples and left.

Hercules was the son of Zeus and Alemene. As such, he grew up in the city of Thebes and received the finest of educations.

Apollo's son Linus taught Hercules to sing and play the lyre, Hermes' son Autolycus taught him how to wrestle, his cousin Eurystheus taught him archery, his brother Castor gave him boxing lessons, and Rhadamanthus, a judge in the underworld, instructed him in understanding and virtue.

Despite these privileges, fortune's cards were stacked against Hercules from the beginning. Hera, furious that Zeus had had another illegitimate child, was determined to undo Hercules. Just after he was born, Hera sent two serpents to strangle him in his crib. To her great disappointment, the extraordinarily strong infant killed the snakes with his bare hands.

Hera plagued Hercules throughout his life. As a young man, Hercules was awarded the hand of King Amphitryon's daughter after fighting with extreme courage in a battle for Thebes. As she looked down at Hercules' wife and children, Hera decided that Hercules was too happy for her liking. She cursed him with madness. Shortly thereafter, in a fit of insanity, Hercules killed his wife, two of his own children, and two of his brother's children. If the goddess Athena hadn't stepped in at that point, the killing might have gone on.

Athena rescued Hercules from himself. With the Gorgon's head that hung from her breastplate, she hypnotized him into a deep sleep to prevent him from committing further murders. When he awoke, his madness was gone.

Hercules' conscience plagued him day and night as he recalled the terrible deeds he had committed. In desperation, he went to the Oracle at Delphi for guidance. The priest at Delphi told him that, as a penance, he must obediently serve his cousin King Eurystheus for twelve years.

With a renewed sense of direction, Hercules eagerly left for Eurystheus' palace. He did not know Hera had greatly influenced King Eurystheus. Eurystheus despised Hercules and sought to humiliate him and conquer his spirit. To this end, the king thought up the twelve most impossible tasks he could. These tasks came to be known as the Twelve Labors of Hercules.

First, King Eurystheus ordered Hercules to kill a lion with his bare hands. After a great struggle, Hercules thrust his arm down the throat of the beast. Eurystheus' second command was that Hercules kill the nine-headed Hydra.

Whenever one of Hydra's heads was cut off, another grew back in its place. Hercules bested the Hydra by setting fire to all but one of its heads. The remaining head was immortal, so Hercules buried it under a stone.

For his third task, Hercules captured a large, swift deer with golden antlers. The fourth labor was to capture a huge boar with razor-sharp teeth, which Hercules accomplished by throwing a net over the snarling creature. For his fifth task, Hercules was sent to wash out stables in which three thousand oxen lived. Because the stables had gone without cleaning for thirty years, this task seemed near impossible (not to mention disgusting) for one man to finish. Hercules accomplished it by damming the rivers Alpheus and Peneus so that they coursed through the stables and cleaned them out.

Hercules' sixth chore was to go to Arcadia and kill the Stymphalian birds. Pets of the war god Ares, the vicious birds had sharp claws, wings like daggers, and feathers they could shoot like arrows. If you confronted them and lost, they ate your flesh.

Hercules called on the assistance of Athena. To get the birds in the air, Athena startled them with a loud rattle. Once the birds were in flight, Hercules shot them with his arrows.

The seventh task was to capture the Cretan bull, a majestic animal that belonged to King Minos of Crete. Hercules managed to corner the bull, grab and tie its legs, and throw it over his shoulders. Hercules carried the Cretan bull on his shoulders to present it to King Eurystheus, and was given an eighth task for his troubles.

The eighth labor of Hercules was to capture the wild, man-eating horses of Diomedes. To do this, Hercules killed Diomedes and fed his flesh to the horses. After eating their master's flesh, the horses became gentle enough to capture. The ninth challenge took Hercules to Asia Minor, where he was to confront a strong race of women called Amazons and return with one of their "girdles" for Eurystheus' daughter Admeta. To Hercules' surprise, the Amazon Queen, Hippolyta, agreed to give him the girdle. At the moment, however, Hera appeared again, this time disguised as another Amazon. Hera convinced the race of women not to give the girdle to Hercules. Angry at Hippolyta's change of heart, Hercules killed the Amazon Queen, taking the beautiful girdle with him.

The tenth task pitted Hercules against a three-headed monster known as Geryon. Geryon and his two-headed dog guarded oxen on the island Erythea, and the Sun gave Hercules an enchanted boat that took him there. Hercules slew Geryon and his two-headed dog, filled the magical boat with oxen, and left the island. The eleventh of the twelve labors was the one in which Hercules had to fetch the golden apples from the garden of Hesperides.

For his twelfth and final labor, Hercules was sent to the underworld to kidnap Hell's three-headed guard dog, Cerberus. Hades, god of the underworld, agreed to let Hercules attempt the capture, but stipulated that Hercules could not use any weapons.

Hercules called on Athena and Hermes for help. With the extraordinary speed granted him by Hermes, and the wisdom and cunning granted him by Athena, Hercules approached Cerberus. A violent struggle ensued, but Hercules overpowered the three-headed beast. Triumphantly, Hercules carried the dog up to earth and Eurystheus. Following the king's inspection, Hercules returned the dog to his underworld post. ☉

Perseus and Medusa

WHEN KING ACRISIUS' daughter Danae was born, the king went to Delphi to consult the oracle.

"It is fine to have a daughter," he said, but will I never have a son who can become my heir?"

"You will never have a son," said the oracle, adding, "There is even worse news."

"What could be worse?" asked Acrisius.

"Your daughter," responded the oracle, "will have a son, and this grandson will take your life."

Although Acrisius tried to dismiss this warning, he became steadily more worried as he watched his daughter grow into a beautiful young woman. In desperation, he had Danae locked in a bronze house that no man could penetrate. He did not take into account, however, that Zeus would certainly have noticed Danae's beauty and that a locked bronze house would not deter him.

Soon Danae gave birth to a son, and Zeus named him "Perseus." Danae artfully managed to keep the child a secret from her father until Perseus was four, but then Acrisius stumbled upon the truth.

"I'll kill them both," said Acrisius to his chief counselor. "Make the necessary preparations."

"My king," said the counselor, "is that wise? You know that the killing of kin is a sin that the gods punish severely. Killing two members of your family would bring terrible wrath upon you."

"Perhaps you're right," said the king, "but it would not be a sin to put them in harm's way."

"In harm's way?" asked the counselor.

"Yes. I'll have my carpenters build a big wooden box. Then we'll put my daughter and her son into the box and cast it into the sea. If they drown, it will be at the hands of the gods, not me."

Dropped into the sea and left to a certain death, Danae and Perseus found that the box floated. Soon it washed up onto the shore in Serplus, where Danae and Perseus were discovered by and welcomed into the home of a childless fisherman and his wife.

As he grew into manhood under the guidance of the fisherman, Perseus became an accomplished fisherman in his own right. All of this made Danae very happy, and they could have happily continued in this fashion, if it hadn't been for King Polydectes' visit to this out-of-the-way area of his kingdom.

Upon seeing Danae and Perseus, Polydectes said to the fisherman, "You have a fine family here; your daughter is lovely."

In fact, Polydectes was quite taken with Danae, who had lost none of her good looks. When it was pointed out that she was the young man's mother, not his sister, it did nothing to cool his ardor. When it came to pass that the king decided to marry Danae, though, he wanted to find a way to get rid of Perseus. It was with this purpose in mind that he tricked Perseus into agreeing to search out and behead the Gorgon, Medusa.

Medusa, once a beautiful maiden whose hair was her chief glory, had dared to vie in beauty with Athena. To punish Medusa for her audacity, Athena divested Medusa of her charms and changed her gorgeous curls into hissing serpents. Medusa became a cruel monster of such a frightful aspect that any living thing that looked on her immediately turned to stone. She decorated the cavern in which she lived with the stony figures of men and animals that had had the misfortune to glimpse and be petrified by the sight of her. Polydectes had every reason to imagine that Perseus would become Medusa's next conversation piece.

Eager to begin his quest but unable to locate Medusa's lair, Perseus asked Athena and Hermes for assistance. Hermes agreed to lead Perseus to Medusa's cavern and gave him winged sandals that he could use to fly

and a magic sword that could be used to cut off Medusa's head.

"That's all fine," said Athena, "but have you thought of how Perseus is to get close enough to Medusa to use the sword? The moment he looks on her, he'll turn to stone. How much use will his flying shoes and sharp sword be then?"

Smiling broadly, Hermes bowed and said, "I leave that problem to you, goddess of wisdom, and I'm sure you already have the solution."

"As it happens," replied Athena, "I do."

Turning to Perseus, Athena said, "Here, Perseus, take my shield. When you approach Medusa, do not look at her directly. Use the shield as a mirror and let her reflection guide your approach."

In the chill, dark cavern, Perseus drew carefully near to the monstrous Gorgon and followed Athena's ingenious advice. With Hermes' sword, he severed Medusa's head from her body with one bold stroke. ❂

Perseus and Atlas

AFTER THE SLAUGHTER of Medusa, Perseus, bearing with him the head of the Gorgon, flew far and wide, over land and sea. As night came on, he reached the western limit of the earth, where the sun goes down. Here in the realm of King Atlas, whose bulk surpassed that of all other men, he chose to rest till morning.

Atlas, who was rich in flocks, had as his chief pride gardens dripping with golden fruit.

Perseus said to him, "I come as a guest. If you honor illustrious descent, I claim Zeus for my father; if you honor mighty deeds, I plead the conquest of the Gorgon. I seek rest and food."

Atlas recalled a prophecy that a son of Zeus' would one day rob him of his golden apples. He advanced towards Perseus with the intention of, at the very least, throwing him out of his palace.

Perseus dodged Atlas, saying, "Since you value my friendship so little, accept a colder gift." Turning his face away, Perseus held up the Medusa's head.

The gigantic Atlas was instantly changed into stone. His beard and hair became forests, his arms and shoulders cliffs, his head a summit, and his bones rocks. Each part increased in bulk until Atlas ultimately became a mountain, with the heavens and all of their stars pressing down on his shoulders.❁

The Sea Monster

CONTINUING HIS FLIGHT, Perseus arrived at the country of the Ethiopians, of which Cepheus was king. His queen Cassiopia, proud of her beauty, had dared to compare herself to the Sea-Nymphs, which made them so furious that they sent a sea monster to ravage the coast and destroy coastal villages. The destruction reached such a state that it was decided that a delegation of elders should accompany King Cepheus on a journey to the oracle at Delphi.

Shortly after arriving, the king stood before the priest and explained his trouble.

"To appease the anger of the Sea Nymphs," the priest announced, "you must chain your daughter Andromeda to the largest rock in your harbor, where she will be exposed to the sea monster's wrath."

"O dear gods!" cried the king. "I'd sooner chain myself!"

Disconsolate, Cepheus returned home to inform his wife and daughter of the oracle's verdict. After many tears and protestations from her parents, Andromeda revealed the courage that ran in her blood.

"What must be, must be," said the princess. "If this is what is necessary to save our people, let us do it and quickly."

Thus it happened that, as Perseus flew over that same harbor, he glanced down and saw Andromeda chained to the rock and awaiting the monster. Flying low, he cried, "Fair maiden, what have you done to deserve this?"

Before Andromeda could speak, a great roar came up from the sea. The monster's head and burst through the surface, and he cut through the waves with his broad breast. Andromeda shrieked, and her parents wailed in from their vantage point on the land below.

"If I save her," Perseus shouted down to Cepheus, will you permit me her hand in marriage?"

The parents immediately and tearfully consented. The monster had come within a deadly range. Suddenly, as when an eagle spies a lizard, swoops down upon him, and seizes him by the neck, Perseus swooped down on the monster and plunged his sword into its shoulder. Stinging from the wound, the monster rose into the air, then plunged into the depths, clawing and thrashing from side to side in agony. Wherever Perseus could find a vulnerable spot between the monster's scales, he struck. He gave the death blow to the monster within minutes.

Cries of joy and relief filled the air as Perseus unchained Andromeda and carried her down to land, where wedding preparations were already being made. ❂

The Wedding Feast

AFTER PERSEUS, ANDROMEDA, and her parents returned to the palace, a wedding banquet was set and guests thronged through the doors. All was joy and festivity until a sudden clamor was heard and Phineus, Andromeda's former fiance, burst in with a gang of thugs.

"Hold!" he shouted. "There will be no wedding here today unless it be for Andromeda and myself. I'll not let an outsider steal what's mine."

Cepheus protested, "Did you claim her when she lay chained to the rock at the mercy of the monster? The death sentence the oracle seemed to pronounce on her as Delphi dissolved all engagements as surely as death itself would have done."

"My arm shall reply," said Phineus, hurling his javelin at Perseus, where it missed its mark and clattered to the ground. Perseus would have thrown his in turn, but his cowardly assailant ran and took shelter behind the altar. Phineus signaled for his supporters to attack the wedding guests, and a brawl ensued.

The old king threw up his hands and cried, "O, gods, witness that I am guiltless of this dishonorable fight! Strike Phineus down—and all others who would intrude on the peace and beauty of this day!"

Perseus and his wedding guests maintained the unequal contest for some time, but the number of assailants was great and their destruction seemed inevitable. All of a sudden, a thought struck Perseus: *I will make my enemy defend me.* With a loud voice he exclaimed, "If I have any friends here, let them turn away their eyes!" Then he held the Gorgon's head aloft.

"Seek not to frighten us with your tricks," said a thug named Thescelus. He raised his javelin but turned to stone before he could throw it. Ampyx was about to plunge his sword into the body of a fallen foe, but his arm stiffened and he could neither thrust forward nor withdraw it.

Astonished at the calamity that had befallen his friends, Phineas called out, "Awaken, dear Thescelus! Force your muscles to move and come to my side! Dear gods, Ampyx is as frozen as a marble statue! Awaken, good friends!"

Perseus laughed grimly. "You waste your breath! Your friends will remain so long after my grandchildren are dead."

"What kind of wicked wizard are you to do such a thing?" asked Phineas.

"Your arrogant attack is responsible for your friends' condition, not me," replied Perseus. "Now it is time for you, too, to pay."

Falling on his knees and stretching out his hands, Phineas turned his head away and wept for mercy. "Take all I have," he begged, "but leave me my life."

"Base coward," said Perseus, "this much will I grant you. No weapon shall touch you. You shall be preserved in my house as an ugly memorial of these events."

Perseus held Medusa's head before Phineus' eyes, and Phineas was no more. ✿

Theseus

THESEUS WAS BORN of a union between Aegeus, King of Athens, and Aethira, the daughter of the King of Troezen. Shortly after Theseus' birth, Aegeus left Troezen to return to Athens. Before leaving, he said to Theseus' mother, "Do you see that large rock in the corner of the palace garden? Under that rock I am going to put my sword and shoes. When my son is old enough to roll the rock away, he is to take the sword and shoes and join me in Athens."

When Theseus reached early manhood, his mother told him of his father's wishes. Eagerly, Theseus approached the rock and easily rolled it back. With his father's sword in his hand and the shoes on his feet, he was ready to proceed to Athens.

"Wait," said his grandfather, the King of Troezen. "The roads between here and Athens are infested with robbers and scoundrels. It is better if you go to Athens by ship."

"No, I shall go by road," said a determined Theseus.

"But I cannot provide you much of an escort," said the grandfather.

"I do not wish any escort," said Theseus, determined to prove himself by taking the more dangerous route. He admired Hercules, whose fame rang through all of Greece, and wanted to work similarly to purge Greece of evildoers and thieves that lurked in the country and preyed on travelers.

On the road, Theseus was at no loss for opportunities to test his courage and strength. Several contests with the petty tyrants and marauders of the country presented themselves, and Theseus was victorious in all. One of the vanquished was called Procrustes, or "The Stretcher." He tied all travelers who fell into his hands to an iron bedstead. If they were shorter than the bed, he stretched their limbs to make them fit it; if they were longer than the bed, he chopped off a portion of their legs. Procrustes, however, was no match for Theseus.

Having overcome all the perils of the road, Theseus at length reached Athens, where new dangers awaited him. The sorceress Medea, who had fled from Corinth after her separation from Jason, had become the wife of Aegeus, Theseus' father. Divining Theseus' identity and fearing a loss of influence over her husband if Theseus should become acknowledged as his son, Medea said to Aegeus, "My lord, there is a young man who wishes to see you. He will speak soft words to you that he learned from a wizard, but that is only to lull your suspicions."

"Lull my suspicions?" asked Aegeus. "For what reason?"

"He wishes to relax you so that he may destroy you."

"Well, send him in. I'll listen to his soft words and have him killed," said Aegeus.

"I believe, my lord, it would be unwise to listen to his words," replied Medea. "He speaks with a sorcerer's bewitching power. Why don't I prepare a fatal potion that will kill him instantly? It will appear that he died from natural causes."

"Fine," said the king. "Prepare the drink and bring in the stranger."

Not long afterwards, Medea, carrying

what appeared to be a bottle of wine, rejoined the King. Theseus knocked at the door and was welcomed inside.

Theseus bowed to the king and his bride, and Medea proposed a toast, passing Theseus a cup of the poisoned wine.

Just as Theseus brought the goblet to his lips, Aegeus spotted the sword the young man carried. He realized instantly that Theseus was his son, and shouted to prevent him from taking a first swallow. Rising from his chair, Aegeus stepped forward and embraced Theseus, while Medea slipped from the room and skipped town. For Theseus and Aegeus, it was a happy reunion, and Aegeus soon named Theseus as his successor to the crown.

The Athenians at that time were suffering greatly because of a bloody tribute they were forced to pay yearly to Minos, King of Crete. Seven Athenian youths and seven maidens were sent to Crete each year to be devoured by the Minotaur, a monster with the head of a bull and the body of a man. The Minotaur was kept in a giant labyrinth so artfully contrived that all who were forced into maze never found their way back out. In this strange home, the Minotaur roamed and was fed on sacrificed humans.

Theseus resolved to deliver his countrymen from this horror or die trying. When the annual time for the tribute arrived, he volunteered himself as one of the human sacrifices. As usual, the tribute ship departed under black sails, and Theseus promised his father he would change them to white on his return to signal his victory.

Arriving at Crete, the youths and maidens were paraded before Minos and his daughter Ariadne. At the sight of Theseus, Ariadne fell deeply in love, and the look in his eyes told her that she was not alone.

Before the human sacrifices were dropped into the labyrinth, Ariadne found an opportunity to slip Theseus a sword that possessed the power to kill the Minter. In his other hand she placed a spool of thread.

"Thread?" Theseus joked. "Am I to sew up the monster's mouth?"

"Hush," whispered Ariadne. "Even if you successfully slay the Minotaur, you could die of starvation before ever finding your way out of the labyrinth. As you walk, let the thread unroll. When you are ready, find your way back to the entrance by following the thread."

The next morning Theseus successfully met and slew the monster, and, thanks to Ariadne, easily found his way back through the labyrinth that had defeated so many others. He met up with Ariadne and they set sail for Athens. On their way, they stopped at the island of Naxos, where Theseus left Ariadne asleep on the shore and silently sailed away. His excuse for abandoning his beautiful savior was that Athena had appeared to him in a dream and commanded him to do so. Theseus' heart was so heavy as he sailed towards Athens that he forgot to change the ship's black sails to white and signify his victory. As a result, the old king, thinking his son had perished in the labyrinth, put an end to his own life. Thus did Theseus become the king of Athens. ❂

Jason And The Argonauts

The Search for the Golden Fleece

"HIGH PRIEST," ASKED King Pelias, "explain this prophecy. Why do I need to fear a man who wears only one sandal?" A mystified and concerned King Pelias stood at the shrine of the Oracle at Delphi.

The voice of the Oracle boomed its answer.

"Pelias, for you stand to die at the hands of a one-sandaled man. He will be your relative"

The lights darkened, and Pelias was left with his own thoughts.

"I will be prepared for this man," thought Pelias, "for I am certain the Oracle speaks of my nephew Jason. Soon, I expect, he will be coming to claim the throne of his father, my half-brother. The throne may be rightfully his, but I will never surrender it. Jason, my nephew," Pelias vowed, "will not take the kingdom of Iolcus from me."

As Pelias stood before the Oracle at Delphi, a handsome young man was standing on a mountaintop many hundreds of miles away. The young man, Jason, had just turned eighteen. Next to him stood a Centaur, a creature with the body of a horse but the chest and head of a man. As a child, Jason had been placed in the care of the Centaur, Chiron, by his father, Aeson, King of Iolcus. Growing up, Jason knew that when the time was right he would return to Iolcus and take over as king. That had been the order his

father had given when ill health forced him to retire. As a temporary measure, King Aeson had appointed his half-brother as King of Iolcus, but when Jason came of age, the throne would be his.

"Chiron, it is time I left to take my place on my father's throne," Jason sighed. Despite his resigned words, emotion clouded Jason's eyes, for both Jason and Chiron were saddened by the fact that they would soon be out of each other's company. Then Chiron spoke.

"May good fortune go with you, my boy. But be careful! Do not expect Pelias to hand over the throne graciously. After all, he has enjoyed that position since your father placed him there seventeen years ago."

With Chiron's words ringing in his ears, Jason set out for Iolcus.

Jason approached his future kingdom in peasants' clothing and a pair of sandals. As he crossed a stream just outside the city, his foot became caught between two large rocks. He pulled the foot free, but lost one of his sandals in the current. The sandal floated downstream and Jason continued on in only one sandal. The sun was sinking as he entered the city.

"This," he said aloud, "is the place where I will reign."

On entering the palace, Jason was greeted with a wide, phony smile from his uncle. Pelias had noticed that Jason was missing one of his sandals. Pelias bade his servants give Jason a luxurious bath and fine food. By the time Jason returned to his uncle, Pelias had a plan.

"I must tell you something that troubles me, nephew," he said. "Years ago, a priest warned me that someone would come to the palace pretending to be Jason, the son of my half-brother. I was told that the impostor would try to learn all that he could from me, then kill me and steal the throne. So, young man, if you are truly the son of my half-brother, you must prove it. The task I am about to give you is one that the priest said only the *real* Jason would be able to perform. To prove your case, you must sail to Colchis and bring back the Golden Fleece. You know of the Golden Fleece, do you not?" finished Pelias.

"Yes, Uncle," said Jason. "I know that many years ago a fleece of pure gold was taken from a sacred, winged ram. This Golden Fleece was stolen by Phrixus and taken to Colchis."

"Correct," said Pelias. "It will now be your task to secure that fleece and return it to its proper place." While he said this, Pelias thought, "I don't have to worry about *that* ever happening. I'll never see young Jason again because he'll never get back here alive."

Jason had no alternative but to accept the mission. Thus began Jason's adventures in search of the Golden Fleece.

Jason built a sturdy ship of sacred wood provided by the goddess Athena. Called the *Argo*, this ship possessed magical powers and was manned by an extraordinary group of men. The *Argo's* crew included Hercules and boxing and wrestling brothers, Castor and Pollux. Jason and the Argonauts were to encounter many challenges in their quest for the Golden Fleece.

One stop in particular proved to be especially harrowing for the adventurers. As they approached an uncharted island, the Argonauts were mistaken for pirates. Fired on when they went ashore, the crew of the *Argo* shot back defensively. The misunderstanding was to end in the death of the king of the island and the wounding of many on both sides. As a result of this incident, Hercules decided not to continue on the quest. Deflated in spirit, Jason and the others sailed on without Hercules.

Soon Jason and the Argonauts landed on an island inhabited by huge, hideous birds called Harpies. If these repulsive creatures didn't kill a man with their hooked claws and sharp beak, they could finish the job with their terrible stench.

Passing a cave on the island, the sailors heard the wails of an old, deposed king who had been cursed and made the hostage of the Harpies. Peering into the cave, Jason gasped at the miserable conditions in which the wretched man lived. As the old king was explaining his situation, a flock of Harpies swooped down with their claws poised to kill. Jason called upon the gods for help, and a booming voice rang down from the heavens.

"Begone, you foulest of birds! By the unconquerable force of the North winds, you are banished from this island forevermore."

The voice belonged to one of the two sons of Boreas, the Great North Wind. With their powerful lungs, they blew the Harpies away on the wind. The old king was now a free man.

Before the *Argo* could reach its final destination, the crew faced one more test. They had to navigate the ship *Argo* between two constantly crashing rocks, the Scylla and the Charybdis, that smashed and sunk many a mighty ship. For their goodness in rescuing the king, Jason and his men once again received the assistance of the gods. With their help, the Argo was able to move safely through the treacherous channel.

"Look, men! It is Colchis!" cried Jason, and the crew looked and saw their hard-won destination. As they made for land, the adventurers couldn't have been more grateful.

Comprehension Check

1. Just about everyone is familiar with the phrase, "The Twelve Labors of Hercules," but few people know why Hercules performed these labors. Identify four of the labors you find the most memorable and state why Hercules undertook these tasks.

2. What was it that enabled Perseus to do his great deeds?

3. What was it that enabled Theseus to do his great deeds?

4. What was it that enabled Jason to succeed in his mission?

CHAPTER 3

THE LOVERS

Jason and Medea

JASON MET WITH the ruler of Colchis, King Eetes, and asked after the Golden Fleece. "There are two conditions under which you will be allowed to leave with the Fleece," Eetes replied. You must first harness the two ferocious bulls that the god Ares keeps in his temple. Once they are bound, you must grab the bag of dragon's teeth that they guard. On your return here, you are to sow the teeth of the dragon like seeds. As each tooth hits the earth, it will immediately turn into a warrior you must vanquish."

Later that evening, after some more conversation, Jason went to bed. He had just fallen asleep when he was jolted awake by the sound of a movement in the room. Widening his eyes, he saw a vision at the foot of his bed. In a moment he realized the vision was an actual woman, and that she was beautiful.

"Fear not, Jason," she whispered. "I am the King Eetes' daughter, Medea. My father has not been fair with you. He is plotting against you. But I can help you perform these seemingly impossible tasks."

Medea explained to Jason that she had magical powers and was willing to use them on his behalf.

Jason was puzzled. "Why," he asked, "do you go against your own father for a stranger? What is my happiness to you?"

Medea had no answer for him. She herself could not understand the great and sudden affection she felt for this man. Little did she realize that a love spell put on her by the goddess Aphrodite had softened her heart towards Jason.

"Here," she said, holding out a jar. "Use this ointment. It will protect you tomorrow against the heat of the flames from their bulls' nostrils." She leaned closer to Jason and whispered something into his ear about the dragon's teeth.

The next day citizens crowded into the sacred grove where the events were to take place. Although not at all sure he could trust Medea, Jason did rub on the heat-deflecting ointment before confronting Ares' fiery bulls. In less than five minutes, he succeeded in getting a harness on the huge creatures and tying them up. The surprised spectators cheered. King Eetes clapped, too, but was clearly confused. "How can this be?" he thought. "Surely these bulls should have killed Jason as they have killed everyone else who has tested them."

By now, Jason had obtained the sack of dragon's teeth left unguarded by the bulls. After a few moments' hesitation, he reached into the bag and quickly began walking and sowing the teeth as directed. As soon as each tooth hit the ground, a fierce soldier sprung up in its place. Eetes expected that the sight of a field fill of warriors ready to attack him would shock and confuse Jason, but he was wrong. As coolly as if he were standing at the helm of his ship, Jason reached into his pocket and pulled out a stone. Smiling, he surreptitiously threw the stone at the largest soldier. This warrior, no doubt the chief of the group, was enraged when he felt the stone pelt his skin. Not knowing from which direction the stone had come, and never suspecting that Jason could have thrown it, the angry soldier turned on the other soldiers.

"Who threw that stone at me?" the soldier bellowed. Before anyone could answer, the big soldier attacked the warrior standing next to him. The soldier next to that one joined in the fight; then the soldier next to *him* did, and soon an all-out battle was raging. When the dust finally settled, not one of the warriors was left standing. King Eetes stood in astonishment at what he just had witnessed.

Having completed both tasks, Jason should now have been given the Golden Fleece. King Eetes, however, attempted to stall the transaction. Once again, Medea offered Jason assistance. She told Jason that the priceless fleece was kept guarded by a ferocious dragon in the palace garden. Later that evening, she led him to the spot.

While Jason had easily handled the bulls and field full of warriors, he took one look at the dragon and gave up. He was not willing to put his life on the line with so little chance of success.

"Jason, wait," said Medea. "That dragon can be our friend. The little fellow is just hungry." She pulled a bit of food from under her robe and tossed it towards the dragon, who quickly gobbled it up. Within minutes, the animal was sound asleep. Jason and Medea tiptoed into the garden, grabbed the Golden Fleece, and fled the palace. Triumphant, they joined the rest of the *Argo's* crew and set sail for Iolcus.

High above, Aphrodite had watched all this with growing unrest. She decided that things had gotten out of hand, and she had had enough of Medea. Aphrodite vowed that she would someday punish Medea for repeatedly betraying her own father.

Quite unaware of the goddess' anger, the lovers sailed for Iolcus. Hoping to discover that their happiness was to last, Medea and Jason stopped at the Oracle at Delphi. There they asked the Oracle if they had anything to fear from King Eetes. The Oracle answered that Jason should fear not Eetes, but a child of Eetes. Believing this warning referred to her brother, Medea devised a plan.

Medea sent a message to King Eetes telling him that she regretted stealing the fleece. She would return it if he would send her brother to meet her secretly. She lied that Jason knew nothing of the letter she was sending.

Eetes, delighted at the thought of getting his Golden Fleece back, called his son.

"You must go now to meet your sister in secret. She writes that you are to meet her in a cave located on the westward side of Mt. Helenus. There she will turn over the Golden Fleece to you. Go now."

Medea's unsuspecting brother left for the rendezvous point. When he reached the cave, Jason sprang out of the darkness and plunged a sword into his heart. Jason and Medea returned to Iolcus with the fleece still in their possession, and with spirits made lighter by the thought that they had outwitted the Oracle's prophecy.

Back in Iolcus, Medea gradually became convinced that King Pelias had something to do with the death of Jason's father. Determined to revenge this death, she became friends with Pelias' daughters. Once she had the confidence of the two women, Medea persuaded them that she could, through her magic, erase years from their father's age and turn the aging king into a young man. Pelias' daughters, who adored their father, believed her and agreed to give Pelias the "youth serum" Medea had concocted. While the king was skeptical as to whether the potion would work, he was not at all suspicious and gamely swallowed it in one gulp. In an instant, he fell to the palace floor. He was dead before his daughters could reach his side.

Pelias' death opened the way up for Jason to assume his rightful place on the throne.

Now Jason had both the Golden Fleece and the kingship. Proudly, he hung the Golden Fleece upon a palace wall.

"This is it," thought Aphrodite. "Medea has gone too far. It is time for the curse to be felt. Medea has cut her own throat; I will wait no longer." Aphrodite began planning a fitting punishment for Medea.

Several years passed, and Jason and Medea gained two sons in addition to power and wealth. Their only problem was that Jason—perhaps as a result of Aphrodite's curse—had developed a wandering eye and a thirst for yet more power and money.

One night as he sat alone, Jason thought, "Although I am King of Iolcus, would it not be better if I were also King of Corinth? If I were to marry the daughter of the king of Corinth, I could easily become the king of that country. If any harm were to 'accidentally' come to the king, I would be next in line for the throne."

He worried, though, how he would handle the situation with Medea. "She has, after all, done so much for me. Also, she is the mother of my two sons."

In the end, however, Jason's thirst for power overrode any concerns about his current wife. Once he set up the arrangements, he told Medea of his decision.

"Jason," cried Medea, "I have sacrificed everything for you. I betrayed my family for you; I stole from my father and killed my own brother for your sake. How could you do this to me? How could you abandon your sons and me for another woman?"

No matter how much Medea pleaded, Jason would not be swayed. In time, he informed her that she and her two sons had to leave the city because her behavior offended the king. The three were forbidden from ever returning. When Jason told her that she need not worry about money because he would provide her an allowance, Medea laughed bitterly and silently vowed she would get revenge. Months later, after Jason's second wedding, Medea sent his new wife a lovely dress. Little did anyone realize that Medea had spun the dress herself and anointed it with a magical potion.

"Who sent me this beautiful gift?" asked Jason's wife, quickly slipping into the new dress. She had just smoothed it down with her fingers when it burst into flames, engulfing the princess in an inextinguishable fire.

Medea, expecting Jason to come after her, hurriedly called her sons to her side, muttering

"He will kill me, but I will kill my children first. Without me to protect them, they could face all manner of evil at the hands of their father. They might even be sold into slavery. I can't allow my sons to suffer."

Then Medea stabbed both of her sons, fittingly punctuating a tale of betrayal, lust, and ambition. ❂

Pyramus and Thisbe

TWO FEUDING FAMILIES lived next door to each other in Athens. So great was the animosity between them that they put up a thick wall to separate their gardens.

A son, Pyramus, was born to one of the families, and a daughter named Thisbe was born to the other. As the children grew, they learned to communicate through secret signs and glances as they passed each other in the street. They became friends, and, by the time they were sixteen, they had fallen in love.

Although their families forbade the two youths from talking to each other, the lovers discovered a small crack in the garden wall. After this discovery, Pyramus and Thisbe spent many starry nights leaning against the wall and whispering about the future.

"Our parents will not permit us to marry," said Pyramus one night, "but they cannot command us not to love."

"But this cruel wall keeps us from loving as we'd like to," moaned Thisbe.

At the end of each night's visit, the lovers pressed their lips against the wall as if they could kiss each other through the stone.

The time came when Thisbe was no longer satisfied with the limited access to her lover that the wall permitted.

"Pyramus," breathed Thisbe, "we must meet face-to-face tomorrow night."

"I know a place by the tomb of Ninas where we can meet," agreed Pyramus. "Near the tomb is a white mulberry tree; it sits next to a clear stream."

The time was set, and all day the young lovers waited impatiently for the sun to drop below the horizon.

That night, a veiled Thisbe whispered Pyramus' name as she crept up to the tomb of Ninas. Her heart racing, she soon found the tree and the clear stream that Pyramus had described. As she sat alone in the darkness, a lioness suddenly approached the stream, its jaws dripping blood from a recent kill.

Thisbe ran and took shelter in the hollow of a large rock, dropping her veil as she went. When the lioness reached the stream, it sniffed at the veil, tearing it and leaving it bloodied by razor-sharp teeth.

Having waited for his family to settle in for the night, Pyramus now approached the meeting place. "Thisbe," he called softly as he approached. He could see the lioness' footprints in the sand, and he blanched as he imagined the danger that Thisbe may have faced. Finally, his eyes lit on the bloody veil. "Sweet love!" he cried. "You have died in trying to meet me. I swear I will not be separated from you any longer!" Staggering, Pyramus propped himself up against the mulberry tree, drew his knife, and plunged it into his heart. Blood splashed onto the mulberries, staining them red.

By this time, Thisbe, still trembling with fear but not wanting to disappoint her lover, stepped cautiously forth from her hiding place. She looked anxiously for Pyramus, eager to warn him about the lioness.

"What is this?" she said as she saw the red mulberries from a distance. "This cannot be the same tree," she said to herself. As she approached, she saw the figure of a youth struggling in the throes of death. A shudder ran through her body as she at last beheld her lover. Holding the near-dead Pyramus, she poured tears into his wound. She kissed his cold lips and said, "Oh Pyramus, what have you done?" She then saw the torn and bloody veil and the knife by his hand. "You have slain yourself thinking I was lost to you," she said. "I, too, can be brave, and my love is as strong as yours. I will follow you."

Thisbe picked up her lover's knife. "As love and death have joined us, let one tomb contain us. And you, tree, let your red berries serve ever after as a memorial of our love."

With that, Thisbe plunged the knife into her breast and died. ✿

Pygmalion

PYGMALION WAS A sculptor and a perfectionist. His discerning eye picked out so many flaws in living women that he came to hate them. "I will never marry," he said, whenever he was asked about his future.

Being alone, Pygmalion had a great deal of time to devote to his sculpting, and one day he surprised himself by sculpting a perfect, flawless woman out of the purest ivory. When he was finished, he looked at his creation and said, "No living thing could ever be as beautiful as you." With its astonishing details, the sculpture almost seemed as if it were alive. Often the sculptor would lay his hand on the statue as if to assure himself that it was not real.

As time passed, Pygmalion began to fall in love with the statue, talking to it as if it were a real woman. "Shall I shut the window?" he would ask, imagining that the statue might be cold. He also began to give the statue presents, as if it were a girl he was interested in marrying. He bought the statue fine jewelry and clothes, putting expensive earrings on its ears and fragrant perfume on its neck. He dressed it in the finest clothes, and by and by, came to think of it as his wife.

In Cyprus, where Pygmalion lived, the annual festival of Aphrodite was being held. When Pygmalion had performed his part in the sacred ceremonies, he stood in front of the altar and timidly said, " O gods, who can do all things, give me, I pray you, a wife like my ivory maiden."

Aphrodite heard Pygmalion and knew what was in his heart when he uttered the prayer. Pygmalion left the festival and returned home, where he greeted his statue in his usual manner. "Hello, my love," he said, and bent to kiss her mouth. To his surprise it seemed to be warm. He pressed his lips again and placed his hand upon her arm. The ivory felt soft to the touch. "Is it possible?" he wondered as he lifted the hand of the once-solid statue. After another kiss, he was sure that his prayer had been answered. He knelt down to thank the gods.

"I am home," whispered the statue as she opened her eyes for the first time. ❂

Echo and Narcissus

ECHO, A BEAUTIFUL nymph, loved the woods where she spent her time playing with her friends and frolicking in the woodland streams and glens. A favorite of the goddess Aphrodite, Echo was afflicted with one fault: she talked too much. Echo was so fond of her own voice that she always tried to have the last word. One day this got her into trouble.

Hera, as she did frequently, had come looking for Zeus in the woods. "I know you are in there, playing with your precious wood nymphs!" Hera called out.

Knowing that everyone would be in trouble if Hera found her husband in the company of the nymphs, Echo planned to distract the goddess from her search. "I will give Zeus enough time to get away," she told her friends.

"Why, you look beautiful today!" Echo said as Hera strode into the forest.

"I know," answered Hera, pounding down the woodland path.

"I can see that life on Mount Olympus agrees with you," Echo said in her brightest voice.

"I know what you are up to," Hera said, "and if you think that you are so smart and I am so dumb, I guess I must teach you a lesson for trying to trick a goddess."

"But I. . ." stammered Echo, "I was only trying to. . ."

But before Echo could finish the sentence, Hera said, "You shall no longer use the tongue with which you tried to trick me. Since you are so fond of talking, you shall always have the last word, but you'll no longer have the power to speak first."

"…power to speak first," Echo echoed.

Not long after Hera had robbed her of this power, Echo spied a beautiful youth named Narcissus hunting deer. She followed close behind him and tried to address him, but no words came. The longer she followed him, the more she loved him, but she could speak no soft words to him. While she waited impatiently for him to speak to her, Echo prepared her answer.

Hearing Echo's footsteps trailing him, Narcissus finally called out, "Who is here?"

Echo replied, "Here."

Scanning the forest and seeing no one, Narcissus called out, " No games! Now, Come."

Echo answered, "Come."

Since no one came, Narcissus called again, "Why do you mock me?"

"Do you mock me?" answered Echo.

Narcissus, becoming impatient, yelled out, "Let us join one another!"

Echo answered with the same words and ran out eager to throw her arms around Narcissus and shower him with kisses. "Get back!" Narcissus yelled. "I would rather die than let a trickster like you have me."

"Have me," Echo said, but all in vain. Narcissus left, and she retreated into the woods with a broken heart. In time, her body began to fade into a shadow, and soon it disappeared altogether. The only thing left was her voice, still ready to reply to anyone who called out. To this very day, Echo always has the last word.

The gods did not overlook Narcissus' cruelty to Echo and other nymphs. One day, a maiden who had tried to attract his attention and failed miserably prayed that Narcissus might learn what unrequited love felt like. A goddess heard the maiden and granted her prayer.

That day Narcissus, hot and thirsty from the hunt, chanced upon a clear pool of fresh water. Stooping to drink, he caught a glimpse of his own reflection. "What a beautiful face!" he said, gazing in awe at his image.

Within a few moments, Narcissus had fallen in love with himself.

"Please grant me one kiss," he said as he leaned toward the surface of the water, but, as his lips touched the water, the image fled. The image returned when Narcissus drew back, and Narcissus asked, "Why do you tease me?" He plunged his hand into the water in an attempt to grab the "nymph," and, once again, the image flew from the water. "The nymph loves me," he cried, "but when I hold my arms out for her, she runs away." His tears fell into the water and disturbed the image. As he saw it depart, he exclaimed, "Stay, please stay! If I cannot touch you, let me at least gaze upon you."

Narcissus spent months mumbling and pleading by the side of the pool. Soon, years passed, and the great beauty that had once charmed Echo began to fade. The nymphs stayed by his side for a time and finally said, "Alas, he is gone." Narcissus died of constant exposure to the elements. As he crossed the Stygian river to join the spirits in the underworld, he looked over the side of the ferry and was reunited with his love for one last time.

The nymphs who had once loved Narcissus mourned him and prepared a funeral pyre, but they could not find his body, because it had wasted away. In its place they found a flower, purple within and surrounded by white leaves. Such a flower is still called a "narcissus." ❀

Cupid and Psyche

THE GODS BLESSED a certain king with three daughters. While two of the young girls were plain, it was clear that the third would become a great beauty. The beautiful daughter was named Psyche, and, as she grew older, the legend of her incredible beauty spread from kingdom to kingdom. By the time she was sixteen, everyone in the world knew about Psyche's goddess-like loveliness.

So great was Psyche's beauty that people came from all over the world just to catch a glimpse of her. One day, the king said, "Farmers are forgetting to plow their fields and milk their cows because they want to see my daughter, who they say is more lovely than Aphrodite herself."

Aphrodite had heard the same things from people who visited her temple, and she was not at all happy about them.

"I must do something about this girl that people claim is more gorgeous than a goddess," Aphrodite said to her son Cupid. Cupid's face turned red with anger at the thought of a mere mortal thinking she was more beautiful than his mother, the goddess of love and beauty.

"Tell me what to do to fix things with this foolish girl, and I'll fly to the task," said Cupid.

Aphrodite, pleased by the reaction of her handsome son, pondered over an appropriate punishment for Psyche. "I can't make her ugly," she thought, "or people will think that I am jealous of her mortal beauty."

After pondering for some minutes, Aphrodite exclaimed, "I have it! Cupid, use your arrows to make Psyche fall in love with the most hated, dirty, vile man that you can find. In that way, she will become as hated and mocked as she is presently loved and worshiped."

"Consider it done," said Cupid over his shoulder as he flew towards earth. Cupid, however, was not prepared for how beautiful Psyche really was. Used to humans' exaggerations when speaking of beauty and love, he gasped in surprise when he arrived at Psyche's bedside and saw her breathtaking face. "It is possible that my mother *does* have a rival in this girl," he said as he crept closer.

At that moment, Psyche opened her eyes and the room seemed to be lit by her smile.

Cupid, surprised, fell backward and jabbed himself with his own arrow. "I am in love with this girl," Cupid said quietly to himself. He knew then that he could not carry out his mother's orders.

Cupid felt confused by this great beauty and the love he bore for her. Although he knew that his mother would be furious at the turn of events, he did not want to lose Psyche to another man. He put some drops of water on Psyche's lips, a charm to prevent anyone else from falling in love with her.

While Cupid plotted to win Psyche for his own, Psyche's mother and father began to worry about their daughter. "My wife," said the king one afternoon, "men come from near and far to see our daughter, but no one falls in love with her."

"I know," answered the queen. "It is as if she is a beautiful vase that people are afraid to touch for fear of breaking."

"While her sisters are married and happy, she, the most beautiful one, is becoming sad and lonely. There must be something we can do," said the king.

"If we have somehow offended the gods, we must go to the Oracle of Apollo and make amends," said the queen.

The king and queen journeyed to consult the Oracle of Apollo in order to get advice and, if necessary, make amends. Before the king and queen reached the Oracle, however, Cupid visited Apollo and told him the sad story. "I am moved by your plight, Cupid," said Apollo, "but Psyche is a mortal and you are not. You know that your mother will not allow this marriage."

"I know," answered Cupid, "but Psyche and I must be together."

Apollo consented to Cupid and Psyche being together, but decided they could only be so at night. In this way, Cupid could keep the marriage a secret. "Make your house ready for your wife, and I will see that your wish is granted," said Apollo.

Later that day, when the king and queen arrived at the Oracle, they prayed for Apollo's help and received a quick answer. "Take your daughter to the mountaintop and leave her there for her husband," said the Oracle.

"Her husband?" gasped the queen, surprised by the baffling news.

"Do not rejoice," boomed the oracle. "Your daughter is to be married to a vile monster, and you shall never see her again!"

In deep sadness, the terrified king and queen hurried away to carry out the Oracle's instructions.

On the day of the wedding, the king and queen walked Psyche to the top of the mountain. "Do not cry, mother," said Psyche. "If I am fated to be married to a monster, than it must be."

As the king and queen left, Psyche turned away, hiding her tears from them. Then a warm breeze caressed her, and she was in the arms of Zephyr, the kindest and most gentle of the four winds. "Do not worry," said Zephyr as he lifted Psyche from the mountaintop, "your husband has sent me for you."

Zephyr set Psyche down in a fresh meadow covered with beautiful flowers. Following a path through the meadow, they came to a wonderful house built of white granite.

"This is the house of a god, not a monster," Psyche said to herself. On entering the house, she became more and more relaxed as she found herself surrounded by the most beautiful fountains and furniture anyone could imagine.

"This is all yours now," said Zephyr as he took his leave of Psyche. "Your husband will be here soon."

Psyche fell asleep on a soft, white bed of down and was awakened in the dead of night by a gentle touch. "Psyche," called Cupid softly, "there are some conditions which our happiness demands."

"What conditions?" asked Psyche, knowing that the voice and the soft touch could not be those of a monster.

"You must never know my name or see me in the light. Our marriage must always exist in darkness alone," said Cupid.

Comforted by Cupid's voice and warm, strong arms, Psyche replied, "It will be as you command."

Thus it came to pass that the two lived together secretly, but in great happiness. As time went on, though, Psyche began to feel lonely during the day while her husband was away. She was also troubled by the fact that she could not see her husband's face in the light. What began as a mystery was becoming an annoyance to the girl.

"May I ever see you in the light of day?" she asked time and again.

"Never," came the constant reply.

"May I see my sisters then?" asked Psyche. "I miss them, and they believe I have married a monster. They are surely worried about my safety."

"If you must see them, I will send Zephyr," said Cupid, "but you must promise

not to reveal anything of our life together."

Psyche promised, and the next day after she woke, she saw her sisters crossing the meadow toward the house. While her sisters greeted Psyche with smiles and kisses, they were inwardly bitterly jealous of their sister's beautiful house.

"Where is your husband?" they asked.

"He is out hunting and will not be back until tonight," Psyche answered. Her sisters were skeptical, and their jealousy drove them to ask question after question until Psyche finally broke down and admitted that she had never seen her husband in the light of day and did not even know his name.

"I'm shocked!" said one sister.

"You know," said the other sister, "he could still be the monster that was prophesied by the Oracle."

"No, he definitely is not a monster," Psyche protested.

But her sisters knew how to wear Psyche down. "How do you know if you have never even seen him?" one asked.

"How do you know he doesn't become a monster when a light is shone on him?" said the other.

Psyche admitted that she had thought it strange that her husband never wanted to be seen in the light, but she continued to insist that he was not a monster.

"You must look at him in the light to be sure," said one sister.

"Yes," agreed the other, "you must bring a lamp and a sharp knife with you to bed. If he is not a monster, you can go back to sleep; if he has the head of a serpent, however, you must cut it off before he eats you."

Psyche tried to put the words of her sisters from her mind, but she began to wonder more and more about her husband as the days went on. Finally, one night while he was asleep, she crept into the room with a lamp and a sharp knife. When the light from the lamp fell on the beautiful and handsome Cupid, the room seemed to glow brighter.

"His beauty is so great that he must be a god," Psyche whispered to herself. Moving a step closer to the sleeping Cupid, she turned the lamp so that his face was fully in the light. His beauty made her weak and caused her to lose her breath. In her weakness, she spilled some of the lamp's oil on the sleeping god's shoulder.

"What is this?" Cupid said, startled out of his sleep. His shoulder had begun to turn red from the burning oil. "Is my wife is here to break her vow and kill me?"

"No, I just—" Psyche stammered.

"Love cannot live with suspicion," Cupid said as he rose from the bed and spread his wings.

It was at that moment that Psyche realized what she had done: married the god of love and lost him through her own foolishness.

As Cupid flew to his mother's house to have his shoulder treated, Psyche thought about how to win him back. "I must show him that my love is true," she thought. "I will never stop looking for him, and my determined search will prove that my love is constant."

Psyche looked for Cupid throughout the world for the next few years. She prayed to all of the gods for help, but none would help for fear of vexing Aphrodite. At last, Psyche decided to seek Aphrodite herself, hoping that the goddess would be kind enough to allow Cupid to return.

Aphrodite, who still burned with hatred for Psyche, had planned to get revenge, but the goddess had no idea that Psyche would come looking for her.

"I laugh at you, mortal girl," said Aphrodite. "You are not fit to be the wife of my son; you are not as beautiful as everyone claims. Only if you were a very hardworking housewife could you make someone a passable bride one day. Now I will test you."

Aphrodite took Psyche to a grain silo where an entire summer's crop was stored. Telling Psyche that all of the grains were mixed together in one huge bin, Aphrodite said, "You must separate all of the corn from the wheat and all of the barley from the millet. You have one night to finish, and I do not want to find even one grain of wheat in the corn bin. Do you understand?"

Psyche did not say anything in response because she was overwhelmed by the chore. She just sat down in a pile of mixed grains, not even trying to begin a task that was certainly impossible.

As it happened, however, some tiny ants in the grain silo overheard the instructions Aphrodite had given to Psyche. The ants were familiar with the story of Psyche's suffering and, with Cupid's urging, decided to help Psyche that night. Before long, millions of ants had arrived and were swarming around the pile of grain. With one grain of wheat or corn in its mouth, each ant moved this way and that, helping to sort the grain into neat piles.

As the sun rose and the last ant had put the last grain of millet in place, Aphrodite entered the silo and fumed, "I know you have had help with this chore, so I will give you a new one!"

After thinking for a moment, Aphrodite said, "Go to the river at the place where the golden rams drink; from that spot, collect some of their fleece for me so that I might spin a golden blanket."

Psyche bowed her head and began moving toward the river. "I know I cannot get the golden wool from the sheep," she said to herself as she moved along. "The rams are bound to stab me with their horns or worse; everyone knows that they kick and bite anyone who comes near them." Little did she know that Cupid was already at work.

On arriving at the river, Psyche looked at the angry rams who were butting heads. As she stood there, she heard a faint voice. It was the voice of the river god speaking through the rustling reeds. "You can get the golden wool if you know how," said the voice.

"I am afraid I do not know how," said Psyche.

"Then come closer and listen carefully," said the voice. "Wait until the rams finish playing in the thorn bush near the river. Afterwards they will go up the hill to sit in the shade of the oak tree. Once they go up the hill, you may safely cross the river, and hanging on the thorn bushes will be enough golden wool for a blanket."

Psyche did as the river god had told her and returned to Aphrodite with her arms full of golden fleece. Aphrodite, unappeased, said, "Now I shall give you a task that no one

can help you with. Take this box with you to the underworld and have Persephone put some of her beauty in it for me." Laughing, she added, "When you return, I will help you get what you deserve."

Although Psyche knew that Aphrodite was laughing because it was impossible for a mortal to return from the underworld, she set out on her journey. It was a journey she knew would be full of danger and one she would be unlikely to complete. Pausing to rest on a rock, she could not help crying, "I am finished!"

"Why do you cry?" a voice said. "So many friends have helped you to get this far. Do you suppose that they will desert you now?"

The voice told Psyche that the whole world knew of the abuse she had suffered at the hands of Aphrodite; if Psyche needed help, she would always find it nearby.

"To get to the underworld and back safely, you must take a few things," the voice continued. "You need cakes for Cerberus, the three-headed guard dog, and a bribe for Charon, the ferryman for the river Styx. Listen carefully and I will tell you how to proceed."

Armed with new hope, Psyche soon found herself in the palace of Hades and Persephone. The royal couple of the underworld listened to Psyche's story and, taking the box Aphrodite had given her, filled it for her.

"I warn you," said Persephone as Psyche turned to leave with the box, "not to open this box but to give it to Aphrodite as it is right now."

"I will do as you say," Psyche said,

thanking Persephone. As Psyche followed the path out of the underworld, however, she began to think about the beauty in the box.

"I will probably see Cupid soon after I arrive on the other side," she said to herself. "I want to look my best when I see him so as to win him back, so I'll take a little beauty from this box."

When she opened the box, something flew out, but it was not a portion of Persephone's beauty. Instead, it was a deep sleep. This sleep clung to Psyche, causing her to fall into a sudden deep sleep right where she stood.

Cupid, who had arranged everything thus far, saw Psyche sleeping and slipped away from his mother to be by Psyche's side.

"My dear Psyche!" he said, gently removing the sleep from her eyes. He then flew with Psyche directly to Zeus.

Zeus reviewed the entire course of events and said, "All of these problems were caused by Psyche's great beauty. It is clear that she is too beautiful to be a mortal; therefore, I will make her a goddess." With that, Zeus called for some ambrosia and bade Psyche drink it. As the draught flowed down her throat, Psyche became a goddess. Her beauty was no longer a threat to Aphrodite. Cupid and Psyche married, and, soon after, Psyche gave birth to a daughter named Pleasure. ❁

Hero and Leander

IN ABYDOS, A seaside town sitting on the Asian side of the Hellespont Straits that separate Asia from Europe, there lived a handsome youth named Leander. Directly across the straits on the European side was the town of Sestos, where Hero, a beautiful maiden and priestess of Venus lived. The two youths were in love, and the fact that the sea separated them caused them much grief.

The sea was not an entirely insurmountable obstacle. Each night, Leander swam across the straits in order to be with Hero, and each night, Hero guided his path across the waters by placing a lighted torch in a tower. One stormy night, though, when the sea was rough and choppy, the wind blew out Hero's torch and Leander lost his way. His strength failed and, finally, he drowned. Leander's body washed ashore on the European side, and Hero discovered it. In a fit of despair, she plunged into the sea and drowned herself. ❁

Comprehension Check

1. Note any similarities you see in the myths in Chapters 2 and 3 and draw a generalization based on these similarities.

2. If a psychiatrist said, "You have a bad case of narcissism," what is the problem? Explain the derivation of the term.

3. The tale of Cupid and Psyche is considered to be allegorical. An allegory is a story in which the characters represent abstract qualities and thus the stories carry a symbolic meaning along with the literal meaning. If Psyche is interpreted to represent the soul (today, as it did then, the word *Psyche* means "spirit" or "soul"), interpret the symbolic level of meaning.

4. Taking the basic plot from "Pyramus and Thisbe," write an outline for retelling that very popular plot in a modern setting.

5. Write an outline for an updated version of the story of Hero and Leander.

CHAPTER 4

FOUR ADVENTURES

King Midas

ING MIDAS, RULER of the island of Phrygia in Northern Greece, once showed great kindness to a stranger for whom Dionysus had a fondness. One rainy morning, Midas and his servants found this stranger in Midas' garden. The man had taken too much to drink and was out cold. Midas told his servants to carry the man inside and put him to bed. For this kindness, both the stranger and Dionysus were grateful, and Dionysus offered to make Midas' greatest wish come true.

"I wish that everything I touch would turn into gold!" said King Midas with great intensity. "Hear me, Dionysus, great god of pleasure; I desire nothing more."

Dionysus granted Midas' wish with a small smile, suspecting that the gift would not give Midas all the happiness Midas expected it would.

At first, Midas was amazed and overwhelmingly pleased with his new power. Her turned his hat, his sandals, and even his cane into gold. Then he went to his kitchen to get something to eat. To his amazement and dismay, all of the food he touched also turned to gold.

"I can't even swallow a piece of bread," he complained. "Everything I touch and every-thing that touches me turns to gold. This is not going to work. I can't eat or drink. How will I live? I'll soon die at this rate. What am I to do?"

Midas panicked and ran to Dionysus in desperation. He told Dionysus his story and begged that his golden touch be rescinded. Dionysus could hardly make out what Midas was saying under all his tears. To make things worse, Dionysus found Midas' blub-bering funny.

"Hush, Midas," he said, choking back a laugh. "I'll tell you how to fix this. My friend, you must have everything you wish to eat carried to the river Pactolus and washed off there. Then, when you touch it, it will not turn to gold."

To this day, it is said that the river Pactolus contains gold fragments that King Midas deposited there.

With the problem of his nourishment solved, one would have thought that all would now go smoothly for King Midas. Unfortunately for Midas, however, he was picked to judge a musical contest between two gods, Apollo and Pan. Midas objected that he could not tell one musical note from another, but that did not seem to matter to the gods. The contest would be held, and Midas would judge it.

On the day of the contest, Apollo played his lyre beautifully. When it was his turn, Pan, who was half-man and half-goat, played an amusing little tune on his flute that was also excellent and sweet.

"Pan," Midas praised, "you played with such skill and grace that I felt as if I were listening to a beautiful songbird. I choose you as the winner of today's contest."

The powerful god Apollo did not appreciate losing, especially to someone like Pan, whom Apollo believed fell far short of him in every aspect. Apollo felt that Midas had made a fool of him.

"Midas will pay heavily for this disrespect," thought Apollo. "I will make him resemble the jackass that he is." With a wave of his hand, Apollo did the deed.

Poor Midas, who had been admiring his appearance in a polished bowl, realized that his face was gradually changing. His ears grew long, and his nose and chin pushed out. He yelled, "O, gods, I look like a donkey! How can I hide myself? No one must see a king looking like this." In the darkness of the night, King Midas managed to locate a seamstress who made him a cap that covered his head and his long donkey ears.

Keeping to his room during the day, Midas successfully hid his deformity. His barber was the only person to know about the king's trouble, and he was sworn to secrecy. The barber faithfully kept Midas' secret until the pressure inside him to let it out became too great. The loyal barber ran outside and whispered the secret into a deep hole. He covered the hole with soil, hoping to keep the forbidden information from spreading all over the kingdom.

Meanwhile, enraged that his plan to embarrass Midas had not worked as well as he had hoped, Apollo said, "I will fix Midas." Aware of the location of the hole containing the secret, Apollo went to it. Standing at the hole, Apollo made weeds designed to give away Midas' secret sprout. This time Apollo found success, and it was not long before everyone in the kingdom had heard of the king's secret. Every time the wind blew, the weeds whispered the news: *King Midas has asses' ears...asses' ears...asses' ears...* ❂

Daedalus and Icarus

REMEMBER THE LABYRINTH that held the Minotaur, and that Ariadne helped Theseus to escape from? It was built by an astonishingly skillful craftsman named Daedalus. With its thousands of twisting and turning passages, the maze seemed to have neither beginning nor end. Like the river Meander, the labyrinth was directionless. Once inside it, no one could tell north from south or east from west.

Daedalus built the labyrinth for King Minos, who had been pleased when the project was finished but became dissatisfied when Theseus found a way to escape from it. King Minos summoned Daedalus to the palace.

"Who knows the secret of how to escape from the labyrinth?"

"No person but myself, sir," Daedalus replied.

"No builders who helped in its construction know the secret?" asked the king.

"Correct," replied Daedalus. "Because the design was too complex for simple builders to figure out, only I know the secret."

King Minos came to the conclusion that only Daedalus could have helped Theseus to escape.

"You will be my guest here in the castle, and the secret of the labyrinth will never again escape," said the king.

King Minos locked Daedalus and his son Icarus in a tower. But Daedalus, refusing to give up hope, began to think about ways to escape.

"Perhaps we can escape by way of the ships that pass in and out of the harbor," Icarus suggested.

Daedalus considered his son's suggestion, but soon determined that Minos had each ship carefully checked before it could leave.

"Anyway," said Daedalus, "how could we get from this tower to the ship?"

Then one day, while looking through the tower's one window, Daedalus said to Icarus, "Minos can control the sea and land, but the

sky is beyond his reach."

"What do you mean?" asked Icarus.

"We will escape through the sky, my son," Daedalus said with a smile.

Father and son began constructing two sets of wings. They tied feathers together with thread and fixed them in place with wax. They worked for days until the wings had gentle curves just like those of a bird. When they were finished, they tried on the wings. Taking a deep breath, Daedalus fluttered his arms and found himself aloft in the center of the room.

"They work, Father!" Icarus cried out. "We are free!"

"We will be soon, my son," said Daedalus.

The two passed the night in keen anticipation of their flight the next day. As Icarus practiced with his wings, Daedalus gave him some last words of advice.

"Remember to keep a middle course, my son," he said. "Too low and the sea spray will clog your wings, but the heat from the sun may melt them if you fly too high."

"Yes, sir," Icarus said impatiently as he turned and fluttered around the room.

On the morning of the flight, as they crept toward the edge of the castle wall, Daedalus' worry was evenly matched by his son's excitement. A slight breeze lifted them up and out toward freedom. The two glided effortlessly on the wings and soon passed Samos and Delos. With each mile that passed easily beneath them, the father and son became more relaxed. As they flew high above the earth, a shepherd, thinking they were gods, leaned on his staff to watch them.

Seeing his son turning and looping in the

sky, Daedalus called out, "Remember to mind the heat of the sun!"

Icarus was enjoying this new power, however, and was soon too far away to hear his father's voice. As he soared ever higher, he did not notice that the wax of his wings was becoming soft. As the blazing sun melted his wings, Icarus continued to wave his arms, but too few feathers remained to hold him aloft in the air.

His father cried out, "Icarus, Icarus, where are you?"

All Daedalus found were a few feathers floating in the water. ❁

Persephone and Hades

WHEN ZEUS DEFEATED the Titans, a family of fire-breathing giants rose up to challenge him. After a great battle, Zeus bested the giants and imprisoned them under Mount Etna. From time to time, the giants, in their struggle to escape, would shake the earth, and their fiery breath would erupt from the top of the mountain.

When Hades heard the first fiery explosion, he thought that his underworld kingdom was being attacked. Calling his servants together, he said, "Make ready my chariot."

Riding swiftly, Hades inspected the outer edges of his kingdom. As he rode past Mount Eryx, Aphrodite noticed him and said to her son Cupid, "What is Hades doing in our realm? He has never before shown any interest in us."

Ignoring Aphrodite and Cupid, Hades rumbled on in his mighty chariot, dashing across the countryside. "This is too much," Aphrodite said, "Hades will pay for his insolence."

"How?" asked Cupid.

"Shoot one of your arrows at Hades," Aphrodite replied. "Even his cold heart will be powerless against love."

Cupid aimed carefully and launched an arrow that squarely hit its target. At that moment, just as Hades was about to return to the underworld, he saw Demeter's daughter Persephone collecting flowers by a stream.

Demeter was the goddess of agriculture and the harvest, and it was she who caused plants to grow and trees to bear fruit. Her daughter Persephone was her inspiration, and as long as they both lived in the world, there was no need for plows because everything was eternally green and fruitful.

"My heart is torn apart by this scene of beauty," said Hades, bringing his chariot to a halt near the stream. "She must be my bride."

As Hades approached Persephone, the mighty god of the underworld cast a black shadow over the stream. This great shadow blocked out all of the sun and frightened Persephone. Seeing Hades approach, she ran, flowers spilling from her arms. "Help!" she cried, but her mother was too far away to hear her calls.

Hades quickly caught the maiden and carried her off in his chariot. When they came to the river Cyan, Hades struck the river bank with his mighty trident and opened a passage into the underworld.

When Demeter realized that her daughter

was missing, she disguised herself as an old woman and began searching for Persephone. Near the stream, she found the flowers that Persephone had left behind. Fearing that her daughter was lost forever, Demeter began to cry. In a state of profound depression, she sat at the spot for nine days. During this time, crops began to fail and flowers to wither. Slowly the apples and pears turned black on the trees, and all of the plants of the world turned brown and dried out. On the tenth day, Demeter heard the voice of an old man talking with his daughter as they walked down the path.

"Enjoy the company of your daughter while you have her," Demeter said, "for I have lost mine."

The old man and young girl, taking pity on Demeter, invited her to their cottage. On the way, Demeter learned that the old man had a son who was very ill.

"I know some charms that may help," she said, approaching the boy. When she took the boy's hand, his pale face grew warm and red, and his lungs pulled healthy, deep breaths once more from the air.

That night, Demeter returned to the boy's bedside and carried him to the hearth. She placed the boy in the fire and began to mold his arms and legs. Seeing this, the boy's mother screamed out, "A witch! Stop her!" She grabbed the boy out of the flames.

"Your love makes you unwittingly cruel to your son," said Demeter, assuming her godly form. "I was about to make him an immortal god. He will not be a god now, but he will be an important man, who will bring the secret of the plow to the world and will teach about

the grains that can be cultivated with hard work."

Wrapping a cloud around her shoulder, Demeter left the cottage to continue her search for Persephone.

Before long, she found the hole Hades had made in the riverbank. Some river nymphs had seen what had happened, but they feared Hades and would not tell Demeter what they had seen.

"We must do something," one river nymph said. She dove into the water, came up with a piece of Persephone's dress, and placed it at the jagged opening created by Hades.

When Demeter touched the cloth, she realized at once what had happened and flew off to request Zeus' help.

"Please interfere on my behalf," begged Demeter. "Persephone is my only daughter. I will not allow any plants to grow or crops to flourish until I have her back."

Imagining the trouble this would cause, Zeus called for his messenger.

"Hermes," he said, " go to the underworld and ask Hades to let Persephone go." In a flash, Hermes was off to do his father's bidding.

Hades had been expecting such a move on Zeus' part. Before Hermes arrived, Hades made sure that Persephone had eaten a few pomegranate seeds, for anyone who eats of the food of the underworld cannot return to earth.

When Hermes reported this news to Zeus, Zeus said, "Persephone has eaten nothing but four pomegranate seeds. Henceforth she shall live in the underworld for four months of the year—one for each seed—but the rest of the year she shall spend with her mother Demeter."

Thus it happened that in the months when Persephone dwelt with Hades in the underworld, nothing grew, and these months became known as "winter." Each spring, when Persephone returned to the earth, Demeter caused flowers to bloom everywhere in celebration of her happiness. ❁

Baucis and Philemon

ONE EVENING, OLD Philemon and his ancient wife Baucis sat by their cottage door, enjoying a calm and beautiful sunset. Having eaten their meager supper, they intended to spend a quiet hour or two in this manner before bedtime. They were soon interrupted by the shouts of children, though, and the fierce barking of dogs in the nearby village. The racket grew louder and louder until it was hardly possible for Baucis and Philemon to hear each other speak.

"Ah, wife," cried Philemon, "I fear some poor traveler is seeking hospitality among our neighbors. Instead of giving him food and lodging, they have set their dogs on him, as is their custom."

Philemon and Baucis were poor. They had to work hard for a living, and their food was seldom anything but bread, milk, and vegetables. Nevertheless, they were two of the kindest, most generous people in the world. They would cheerfully have gone without their dinners rather than refuse a traveler's request

for food. They frequently offered a slice of brown bread, a cup of new milk, and a spoonful of honey to any weary traveler who chanced to knock at their door.

Unlike Baucis and Philemon, the people of the village were selfish and inhospitable. These villagers had neither pity for the poor nor sympathy for the homeless. They even instructed their children in their own cruel ways, clapping in encouragement when they saw their little boys and girls running after a stranger, shouting at his heels, and pelting him with stones. The villagers also kept large, fierce dogs, and whenever a traveler dared to show himself in the village streets, a vicious pack of them charged to meet him, barking, snarling, and baring their teeth.

"I've never heard the dogs so loud!" marveled Philemon.

"Nor the children so rude!" answered his wife. They sat shaking their heads while the noise came nearer and nearer. Then, at the foot of the little hill on which their cottage stood, they saw two travelers approaching. Close behind them came the fierce dogs, snarling at their very heels. A little farther off, a crowd of children sent up shrill cries and threw stones.

"You go meet the travelers," said Baucis, "while I go inside. I'll see what we can get them for supper. A bowl of bread and milk would do wonders toward raising their spirits."

With this, she went into the cottage. Philemon went forward and extended his hand in a friendly greeting. In the warmest tones he said, "Welcome, strangers! Welcome!"

"Thank you!" replied the younger of the two. Despite his weariness, he managed to inject a bit of liveliness into his voice. "This is a better greeting than we met with in the village. Pray, tell me—why do you live in such a hostile neighborhood?"

Philemon was glad to see his visitors in such good spirits. You would not have guessed by the travelers' looks and manners that they were weary with a long day's journey.

"I, too, used to be light-footed in my youth," he said to the travelers. " I remember how I always found that my feet grew heavier toward nightfall."

"There is nothing like a good walking staff to help one along," answered the younger stranger. "As you can see, I'm lucky to have an excellent one."

This staff, in fact, was the oddest-looking one that Philemon had ever seen. It was made of olivewood and had something like a little pair of wings near the top. Two carved snakes twined themselves about the staff. They were so skillfully carved that Philemon almost thought they were alive. He believed that he could see them wriggling and twisting.

"An odd piece of work, sure enough!" said Philemon. "A staff with wings." By this time, Philemon and his two guests had reached the cottage door.

"Friends," said the old man, "sit down and rest yourselves here on this bench. My good wife, Baucis, has gone to see what we have to offer you for supper. We do not have much, but you are welcome to whatever we have in the cupboard."

"Was there not," asked the younger stranger, "in ancient times, a lake covering the spot where the village now stands?"

"Not in my day, friend," answered Philemon, "and as you can see, I am an old man. There were always the fields and meadows, just as they are now, with the tall trees and the little stream running through the valley. Neither my father nor his father before him ever saw it otherwise, as far as I know. Doubtless it will still be the same when I myself am gone and forgotten!"

"That is more than can be safely foretold," observed the younger stranger sternly, shaking his head. "If the people of that village have forgotten how to be kind and hospitable, it is better that the lake should be rippling over their homes again!"

The younger traveler's frown seemed to grow suddenly darker in the twilight, and Philemon was afraid. When the stranger shook his head again, there was a roll of thunder in the air. ❁

Comprehension Check

1. We left the final paragraph off the story "Baucis and Philemon," but if you've read it carefully, there are clues telling you how it will end. Maintaining the voice and style of the story, write an appropriate concluding paragraph.

2. The tale of Proserpine and Hades is also an allegory. Keep in mind that Ceres is the goddess of agriculture. If, as it is generally assumed, her daughter Proserpine is a symbol for grain seed, what is the symbolic level of meaning in this story?
    You may want think of Proserpine's return to the darkness of Hades in terms of the life cycle of a seed.

3. What obvious point could be drawn from the story of Daedalus and Icarus?

4. Dionysus, the god of wine and good times, is known by the Roman name Bachus. If a gathering of people were described as a bacchanalia, what do you suppose the gathering was like?

CHAPTER 5

THE ROYAL FAMILIES
OF ANCIENT GREECE

The House of Atreus

RETURNING FROM THE grueling Trojan War, King Agamemnon was about to come face to face with tragedy—the seeds of which were planted long before he ever left for the battle. You may remember that Agamemnon was also plagued by misfortune as he prepared to depart for Troy ten years earlier. An incessant series of illnesses, accidents, and storms kept forcing him to put off his departure.

Desperate to know the reason behind all this misfortune, Agamemnon employed a soothsayer.

"Artemis, the goddess of the hunt, is furious because you killed one of her sacred hares," explained the soothsayer. "She is directing troubles and powerful winds against you and your fleet as a punishment."

"But my men and I are fast running out of food and water! Many in my army have fallen ill. What can be done to persuade Artemis to end this torment?" asked Agamemnon.

The soothsayer told the troubled king that Artemis' rage would only let up if Agamemnon sacrificed his daughter Iphigenia to her. Agamemnon was overcome with grief. Feeling he had no choice, he dutifully carried out the wishes of the angry goddess. After being slain on the altar, Iphigenia was given up to Artemis. Upon hearing of Iphigenia's death, Clytemnestra, her mother, was filled with sickness and rage. She cried out, "My Iphigenia, oh, my poor beloved daughter! Of my four children, you were the one dearest to me. Murdered by your own father! O, gods, what hope is there for my broken heart? How could Agamemnon have sacrificed his own daughter? He shall pay for his crime—I swear it by all that is holy!"

Throughout the ten years of the Trojan war, Clytemnestra fed on her anger and grief and waited for a change to avenge Iphigenia's death. Finally, news of the end of the war reached her. She also learned that

Agamemnon was returning with a beautiful slave named Cassandra, the daughter of King Priam. The news of Agamemnon's unfaithfulness further fueled Clytemnestra's anger. Knowing that she needed to act quickly before Cassandra usurped her place, she vowed, "A marriage with Cassandra will never happen. Agamemnon will pay for the murder of my Iphigenia. He will pay with his life...and so will his young lover."

Clytemnestra began planning the deaths of Agamemnon and Cassandra.

"I will have a reception for them when they arrive. It will appear to be some kind of 'welcome home' party."

Unbeknownst to Clytemnestra, however, Cassandra had the gift of seeing into the future. Pacing in her cabin on the ship, she said aloud, "O! Something is trying to warn me not to go to Agamemnon's palace because an evil lurks there. What is it? Agamemnon only laughs when I tell him about such forewarnings. He says they are womanish fears. If only I could see our future more clearly!"

As hard as she tried, though, Cassandra could not unravel the dreadful knot of foreboding that troubled her mind.

When the ship docked, a great victory banquet was held, in accordance with Clytemnestra's plans. A huge crowd collected outside the palace to welcome home and salute King Agamemnon and his men for conquering the Trojans. The commoners hoped that the king would appear on the balcony and speak to them, and were prepared to spend the night in order to catch a glimpse of him.

Inside the palace, Agamemnon and Cassandra enjoyed the party as they sat side by side at the dinner table. As the evening progressed, Clytemnestra made an excuse to leave the table, slipped behind Agamemnon, and drew a dagger from the folds of her gown. With one quick movement, Clytemnestra plunged the dagger into her husband's back. Then she turned and did the same to Cassandra, who managed to say, "No one would listen to me..." before slumping over the table.

Clytemnestra went immediately to the balcony where she explained to the amazed crowd what she had just done. At first the people were livid, but Clytemnestra gained their sympathies when she reminded them of how Iphigenia had died at the hands of the king. She did *not* tell the crowd that with Agamemnon out of the way she was now free to marry her lover Aegisthus. The two did end up marrying, and for a while they lived quite peacefully.

Trouble, however, was brewing. Electra, the younger daughter of Agamemnon and Clytemnestra, was enraged by the news of her father's death. As the result of an argument with her mother, Electra had been living in poverty outside the palace walls for several months. Electra's only hope was that her brother Orestes would return and avenge the death of their father.

To Electra's good fortune, she was not alone in her anger. The god Apollo shared her rage. Appearing before Orestes, Apollo said, "Orestes, you are the only surviving male member of your family. As such, you must punish the person responsible for your father's murder—even though it is your mother who committed the deed. Avenging your father's death is the only way to remove the curse from your family. Let it be known to all that the House of Atreus will not be at rest until Agamemnon's murderer has been punished."

Apollo's words weighed heavily on Orestes' heart, for Orestes loved his mother as much as he had his father. He knew, however, where his duty lay, so he resolved to do as Apollo had commanded and headed for the palace to avenge his father's death.

As Orestes approached the gates of the palace, Electra called out his name. She had been there for three days awaiting his return.

"Orestes, I swear to you, I have not missed a day in front of our father's tomb. I've been praying that you would return and restore honor to our family."

"It has been so long since we have seen each other," said Orestes. "How did you recognize me?"

"By the medal you are wearing around your neck. It is exactly the same as the one that Father had the silversmith make for me."

Sensing Orestes' turmoil, Electra continued, "I understand how terrible you must feel about this. As bad as mother's treatment of me has been, I still regret what has to be done...but we both know what must be done, don't we?"

Orestes sadly agreed, and brother and sister began to draw plans for killing Clytemnestra and Aegisthus. That evening, Orestes visited the palace. Knowing that his mother would be occupied elsewhere, he went directly to Aegisthus' room. Standing silently before Aegisthus' door, Orestes listened for a moment but could hear no sound. Finally, he heard a cough. "Well, someone is in there," he said quietly, "and it appears that he is alone. I pray it is the adulterer Aegisthus." Withdrawing his knife, he knocked on the door with his other fist.

In a moment, the door opened, and Aegisthus stood there with a questioning look on his face. Swiftly Orestes struck. "This is for you, Aegisthus," Orestes muttered breathlessly as he stabbed him to death. Orestes then took his bloody dagger and went looking for Clytemnestra. As he walked down the hall, one of the servants who witnessed the stabbing began to scream. Upon hearing the screams from one of her servants, Clytemnestra came quickly down the hall from the other direction and saw Aegisthus lying dead on the hallway floor.

"Quickly, go fetch a sword. Quickly," she fearfully ordered the servant. In a moment, the servant returned with the weapon. It was at that moment that Orestes reappeared. His sword was still dripping with Aegisthus' blood.

"Stop!" she said. "I am your mother. You are my flesh and blood. Do not force me to kill you. There have been too many deaths in this family already." Despite Clytemnestra's pleas, Orestes could not be turned away from his task. Walking slowly toward her, he raised his dagger ready to strike a lethal blow. In a moment, he would step within the reach of his mother's sword. Just at that precise moment, Clytemnestra released her weapon, and it fell to the floor with a clatter. She allowed herself to be slain by Orestes, rather than kill her son.

Once the deed was done, Orestes was filled with guilt and remorse. "How could I have committed such a terrible deed? How could I have murdered my own mother?" cried Orestes in deep despair. Suddenly, a group of frightful looking creatures called the Furies swooped down, shouting insults at Orestes. These horrible-looking, ghastly females were like birds, had hair made of snakes, and used huge wings. Screeching and screaming, they taunted and abused him. The Furies told him that they had been sent by the gods in order to punish Orestes for committing an unpardonable sin. Day after day, the Furies tormented the guilt-ridden Orestes in this fashion. Finally, the goddess Athena felt pity for Orestes. This came about when he cried out to her, "Athena, I am to blame for everything. The guilt is all mine. Apollo might have instructed me to kill my mother, but I acted on my own."

"Orestes," the goddess Athena said, "you are forgiven for all of your sins. You acted courageously in accepting the responsibility for what you did. All is forgiven; now forgive yourself." With these words she called a halt to the harassing taunts of the Furies, thus ending the curse that had plagued the House of Atreus. ❀

The Royal House of Thebes

Oedipus

ONE NIGHT AS he was walking home, a poor shepherd was startled to hear the cry of a baby. Walking toward the sound, the shepherd discovered a tiny baby.

Amazed, he said, "Who is this poor infant boy? Who would abandon such a baby? Who would leave it on a cold, windy mountaintop to die?"

As he looked closely at the infant, a puzzled expression came over the shepherd's face. He exclaimed: "Who in this world would pierce the feet of a baby?" Bundling up the baby, the kindly shepherd carried the infant down the mountain. As he walked, he thought aloud, "I must get this infant to safety and shelter. What if I hadn't come along? The poor child would have faced certain suffering and death." Thus it was that a simple shepherd saved the life of one of the most famous king in ancient Greece – King Oedipus.

The story rightly begins in the royal palace of Thebes. There King Laius and Queen Jocasta lived quite happily. In fact, things could not have been better except for one small concern. Looking up from his dinner one evening, King Laius said, "This castle needs a baby boy; we need a son and heir."

"I agree, my lord. It would be nice to have a son. A child around here would make the royal household a truly joyful place," exclaimed Jocasta happily.

"I will speak with the Oracle at Delphi on the matter. The gods are sure to agree," said King Laius. For this purpose he journeyed to Delphi the next day, where he questioned the Oracle about the wisdom of having a son.

No sooner had he finished his question, however, than the god Apollo spoke through the voice of the priest. The priest said, "King Laius, a son should not be born to you!"

"But why can't my wife and I have a child

of our own? Why should we not have a son and heir?" asked King Laius. He was deeply puzzled.

"If you have a son, he will murder you and marry your sweet Jocasta. This is the awful truth of the matter. Heed my fatal warning." Needless to say, the Oracle's response sent cold chills up the spine of the king. When he returned home and told Jocasta of the Oracle's warning, both agreed to forget about having a son.

For years, everything went smoothly at the royal household, but then a son was born to Laius and Jocasta. As happens in life, they had not planned to have a child, but nevertheless, a child was born. For weeks they worried and argued about the Oracle's predictions. Finally Laius said, "Jocasta, the child must die. I will have him carried away and left to die in the wilderness. It is either that or we face the most unbearable of tragedies." Jocasta, as a mother will, wept and cursed her misfortune but in the end agreed to surrender her own flesh and blood. Feeling there was no alternative, the parents handed the infant boy to a servant. The servant, after piercing the baby's feet, carried the infant to a mountaintop. Here he set the child down.

In time, King Laius and Queen Jocasta managed to put the incident behind them, and their lives had returned almost to normal. Little did they think that the infant son they had left would be found by a kindly shepherd; nor could they have guessed that this shepherd would carry the infant to the palace of the King of Corinth. They could never have imagined that King Polybus, a kind and loving man, would accept the infant and raise him as his own son. The boy, now named Oedipus, grew into a strong, handsome young man. He was, of course, not aware of the identity of his real parents.

One day many years later, King Laius went on a trip to Delphi. As the he was returning home with four of his friends, fate caught up with him. On a lonely road this group of five travelers got into an argument with a stranger. When the dust settled, the king and three of those with him had been killed by the unknown man. The fourth man managed to escape and returned home to report the sad news. Then, fearing for his own life, he fled the city. The kingdom of Thebes, draping itself in black, mourned for their dead king.

Some short time after this, Thebes fell under the spell of an evil Sphinx and a great misfortune descended on the city. The Sphinx refused to let anyone who could not answer its riddle pass through the great gates of Thebes. It had the head of a woman and the body of a lion, from which a massive set of wings grew. The unfortunate people of Thebes believed that the Sphinx had been sent by the gods to curse them with starvation and suffering. For many years, no one had been clever enough to answer the riddle of the Sphinx, who killed and ate all who approached the gates and failed.

At his home in Corinth, Oedipus had heard about the curse and the horror that had come to the city of Thebes. Feeling that he had little to lose, the handsome young man decided to travel there and offer what assistance he could. While packing for the journey, Oedipus talked with his friend Stamos, saying, "As long as I am alive my father Polybus faces the threat of death at my hands. Because I have nothing to lose, I can afford to go to Thebes and try my strength and cunning against the Sphinx. As you well know, Stamos, the gods have foretold that I will one day kill my father. This is why I must leave Polybus' kingdom." As he said this, Oedipus put the last of his possessions into a sack.

"Oedipus, you are a fool," said Stamos. "None of this makes any sense. You haven't killed your father in all this time, so why would you commit this horrible crime now? It makes no sense for you to sacrifice your life just because of a silly prediction. Look at you; you have moved from place to place, staying as far away from your father as possible. This is a ridiculous way to behave."

Oedipus, with tears in his eyes, said, "I love him, Stamos. But if the gods say I will kill him, I need to be careful. They never said I would *willingly* kill him—it could happen in a fit of insanity

"Frankly, I think you must have decided to challenge the Sphinx in a fit of insanity. But I can see I won't change your mind. Good luck to you on your journey to Thebes," said Stamos.

Within a month, Oedipus found himself standing at the gates of Thebes and facing the Sphinx. The Sphinx said, "So, Oedipus, you wish to play my game. What a foolish and arrogant young man you must be! Well, as the gods wish it, so will it be. You know, do you not, that to gain entrance to Thebes and to save your life, you must give me the correct answer to the riddle I'm going to ask you?" The Sphinx's grin was evil.

"I am here to break your hold upon Thebes, whatever the risk. Ask me the riddle," said Oedipus, eager to accept the challenge.

"Insolent youth!" said the Sphinx. "Here is my riddle: what creature walks on four feet in the morning, two feet at noon, and three in the evening?"

After pausing a moment to think, Oedipus answered, "Man! He crawls at the beginning of life, walks in the middle, and uses a cane as a third foot in old age."

The Sphinx let out a terrible shriek, threw herself from the gates, and died. Oedipus had solved the riddle no one else could, and he received a hero's welcome in the streets of Thebes. That evening, as a reward for his courage and intelligence, Queen Jocasta offered to share the throne of the kingdom with Oedipus. Finding her beautiful, Oedipus happily accepted this honor.

With Oedipus as king, Thebes prospered as never before. In six years, the royal couple had four children, two boys and two girls. For many years after, good fortune continued to smile both on Thebes and the royal family. Then the time arrived when a dark curtain began to descend. All that had passed before was merely the backdrop for the misfortune to follow.

Without warning, famine and disease once more stalked the streets of Thebes.

"For the life of me," Jocasta said, "I can't understand this change. Why has ill-fortune returned to Thebes? Our crops have failed, and disease is killing our livestock! What offense could have earned us this misfortune?"

Oedipus, just as bewildered as his wife, admitted that he had no answer.

"Perhaps," said Oedipus, "we should peak with the Oracle of Delphi."

Oedipus sent Creon, his wife's brother, to Delphi to search for some means that might allow the city to escape its growing misfortune. With the return of the first full moon, Creon returned with a message from the Oracle. The voice of the god Apollo had told him that a crime committed a very long time ago—the murder of King Laius—had gone unpunished. This was the reason the terrible curse was put on Thebes. This curse would remain, the voice said, until the person responsible for murdering the king came forth and punished himself.

With this information in hand, Oedipus was determined to root out the murderer in this almost forgotten crime. He called to the palace a famous soothsayer, Tiresias. Tiresias was blind, but he saw more than many do. He agreed to try to discover the name of King Laius' killer. For the first time in months, Oedipus and Jocasta felt a sense of relief, believing that, with Tiresias' assistance, the curse would now be lifted. In a very short

time Tiresias reported back to them, but all he said was, "Ill-fate and tragedy are set for the man who seeks the truth." Although Oedipus and Jocasta begged him, he would say no more.

Naturally, this angered the royal couple. Oedipus said, "You have told us nothing. You are supposed to know the name of the person responsible for King Laius' death. Tell me, you fool!" When Tiresias refused, Oedipus threatened, "Either you give me the name of the person responsible for the crime, or I will have your head. What is it to be, old man?"

Tiresias said dully, "Your majesty, you are the murderer of King Laius."

"Get out! Get out, you crazy old fool! Get out of here!" shouted Oedipus. He had his guards lead the blind old man from the room.

The darkest gloom settled upon Oedipus and Jocasta. Their hopes for a quick end to the curse were shattered. Oedipus asked, "Could there be any truth in Tiresias' statement? Could I have, as a young man, somehow killed King Laius without knowing it? Tell me what you think, Jocasta. How was Laius killed?"

"No, it is not possible that you killed Laius," she said. "He and three others were killed by a robber on the road. It happened as he was returning home from Delphi."

"Where on the road," interrupted Oedipus, "did it happen?"

Jocasta answered, "In that spot where the three roads meet. This proves that Tiresias sometimes does get things wrong."

Oedipus' face went suddenly dark with a new concern. He asked, "When did this robbery take place?"

"It happened," answered Jocasta, "some months before you arrived in Thebes. There was a fourth man with my husband, but somehow he managed to escape. If he had not escaped, I guess we would never have discovered what had happened," Jocasta explained.

"I want that man found and brought here right away," Oedipus said gravely.

Guards were sent to all parts of the kingdom and soon a frightened old man stood before Oedipus and Jocasta. No sooner had he laid his eyes on Oedipus that he began to scream, "He is the one! That is the man who killed the king! That is him!"

Sinking his head in gloom, Oedipus said, "It is possible that I was the one who killed King Laius and those men. I was at the spot in the roads you described, and I did fight with and kill four men. They had attacked me because I would not get off the road and make way for them. I was protecting my life," Oedipus said.

"It cannot be the same fight," said Jocasta. "You cannot be Laius' killer. The god Apollo told us that Laius would be killed by his son. You, Oedipus, are the son of King Polybus, not King Laius' son. I should know," explained Jocasta. She was confident that this statement would remove Oedipus' deep concern, and Oedipus did, in truth, seem a little relieved.

Later that evening, a messenger arrived from the city of Corinth. He had come to tell Oedipus that his father, King Polybus, had died of natural causes. "Your majesty," continued the messenger, "there is also a message the king wished me to give to you. On his deathbed, King Polybus made a confession. He said that although you are not his natural son he loved you as much as he could love anyone. He regrets that he kept from you the fact that you were adopted. You were discovered on a mountaintop by a shepherd and brought to his castle as an infant."

Jocasta was the first to understand the implications of this information. Paling, she ran wailing from the room.

"We are all doomed," said Oedipus, "Jocasta, my children, and myself. I do not deserve to live." With this, he got up and slowly left the room. In great agony, Oedipus went looking for Jocasta. He thought that perhaps a suicide pact would resolve their pain and suffering. In her chambers, however, he found Jocasta hanging from a beam by a scarf, dead. Now, he felt, death was not a severe enough punishment for him. Raising Jocasta's brooch to his face, Oedipus gouged out his own eyes. With only a staff and a beggar's bowl, the blind Oedipus walked out of the palace.

Because Oedipus' children were not considered legitimate, Creon was made Regent of Thebes. Forced to do so by the elders, Creon exiled Oedipus to Colonus. In this place, created for those suffering from guilt and seeking forgiveness, Creon hoped that Oedipus would find forgiveness for his sins.

Oedipus lived alone at Colonus until his death. After the funeral, because his body disappeared from Colonus, some said that Oedipus had been carried away by the gods so that he might at last find peace. ❂

Antigone

EVEN AFTER OEDIPUS died, the curse was not lifted from the House of Thebes. Oedipus' children—Polyneices, Eteocles, Ismene and, Antigone—were also doomed to meet with tragedy.

After Oedipus stepped down as king, the people of the city offered Creon, the brother of Jocasta, the job of Regent of Thebes. Although not eager to do so, Creon accepted the position. Because they were the children of that ill-fated marriage between Oedipus and Jocasta, Oedipus' sons Polyneices and Eteocles were considered to have been unlawfully born and not worthy to govern.

The two men, however, were determined to claim the throne. They assembled an army and declared war on Creon and his government. In this revolt, the brothers successfully overthrew Creon. It was because of this that Thebes was once again plagued with famine, disease, and death.

"You, Uncle Creon, are no longer Regent. As the victor in war, I will reign as King of Thebes. Thus, I shall ascend the throne and take the place of my father," said Eteocles. It was without any outcry from the people that Eteocles and Polyneices ordered Creon out of Thebes. They forbid him from ever returning to the city again.

"Hurrah! Hurrah! Hail to the new King of Thebes!" exclaimed Antigone. She and Ismene were glad that their brothers were now the rulers of Thebes. The crowd that had gathered at the ceremony was also cheering wildly, though more out of gratitude than enthusiasm for Eteocles. The city of Thebes

had been so devastated by civil war that everyone was relieved that peace was finally at hand. It would not last long.

The gods, in their lust to punish Thebes, now pitted Eteocles and Polyneices against each other in battle. A war, fought by the armies of the two brothers, nearly wiped out what remained of the city's population. The brothers decided to meet in one-to-one combat for the throne. It would be a fight to the death, and the victor would rule Thebes.

When the fighting began, Antigone and Ismene, along with most of the remaining population of Thebes, painfully watched. The crowd gawked at the display of courage and skill by the two brothers, but the battle was brief. In the end, both Eteocles and Polyneices were dead, and the startled spectators slowly backed away from the bodies of the two slain brothers. Filled with incredible pain and sorrow, Antigone and Ismene went from one brother to the other. Then guards came and dragged away the bodies of Eteocles and Polyneices.

As both brothers had been killed, Creon returned to Thebes, this time to become its king. At the urging of his advisors, Creon issued a proclamation: "Polyneices shall be punished for the invasion he led against the City of Thebes. For this crime he will not receive a proper religious burial."

"But, Creon, my lord," said Antigone, "my brother Eteocles will be buried inside of Thebes. Why can you not see fit to do the same for his brother?"

"Please, dear uncle," added Ismene, "Polyneices will have no calm nor peace for his soul if his body is not laid to rest." This was the belief of the ancient Greeks.

"An example must be made of those who stir up civil unrest," said Creon. "Eteocles could have been the one not buried as easily as Polyneices," said Creon. "Don't you understand that the people want to see someone punished for the misery brought on by the civil unrest? Your brother Polyneices does not deserve a proper burial. As far as I am concerned, the issue is settled."

Creon ordered the guards to take Polyneices' body to the outskirts of the city. "Take the body," he directed them, "to an unknown location. There Polyneices' remains can be preyed upon by vultures and wild dogs. It is what he deserves."

To be sure that Polyneices did not receive a proper burial, Creon issued a second decree, which stated that anyone who was caught near the body of Polyneices would also be put to death. Creon's decree furthered angered Antigone, because she was determined to give her brother a proper burial. With this idea in mind, she went out one evening during a whirling dust storm. Cleverly avoiding the guards at the site, she bravely buried her brother's body.

When this act of rebellion was reported to Creon, he went into a rage.

"Who is responsible for tampering with the body of Polyneices?" asked Creon angrily of the guards who had been posted at the location. "If no one comes forward or if you can not tell me who the person is, I shall put you all to death."

On hearing this, Antigone, with Ismene pulling at her to prevent her from stepping forward, fearlessly declared, "I, your majesty, am the person responsible for burying my brother's dead body. I, and I alone, did it. It was last night during a dust storm while everything was covered in darkness." Antigone then cast a stern look toward Ismene, who wanted to claim some of the blame. "No, Ismene, I acted alone. You see, you chose to live; I to die."

Creon liked Antigone and did not wish to carry out the punishment he had decreed. He tried to persuade her to retract her confession. Antigone, however, would not, and her stubborn refusal left Creon with no other choice. Antigone was sealed in a cave and left to die.

Ismene left Thebes and was never heard from again, but Antigone's death ended the tragic curse that had been put upon Oedipus forever. ❀

Comprehension Check

1. Choose a section from either selection and write two pages of dialogue that represents what is taking place on stage. For example, from the "House of Atreus" you could take some paragraphs and write dialogue between Agamenon and those who greet him on his return home; for example, you might construct dialogue between Agamenon and Clytemnastra, dialogue between Clytemnestra and Aegisthus, or dialogue at the dinner table.

CHAPTER 6

THE TROJAN WAR
AND ITS AFTERMATH

The Trojan War

"PESTILENCE IS CAUSING many in my army to become ill and die," wailed King Agamemnon. "God Apollo, I repent. I will return Chryseis to her father; but please, I beg you, end the suffering that has come upon my men and me." After he said this, Agamemnon paused and added, "And, if you see fit, please allow me another beautiful woman to replace Chryseis."

Having captured her during a battle in the Trojan war, Agamemnon now sent Chryseis back to her father.

Unfortunately, the woman Agamemnon selected to replace Chryseis had already been claimed by the brave hero Achilles. Furious at Agamemnon for stealing his lover, Achilles stripped off his armor and vowed that he would not return to the battle. Then the goddess Athena appeared before her son.

"You are quite right to refuse to fight in Agamemnon's army, Achilles. How could we ever have helped someone who shows his appreciation for it like this? I, too, am furious with Agamemnon."

Athena stalked off to Olympus to see if there was something Zeus could do to help Achilles, who was her favorite son. She hoped to get Zeus to turn the tide of war against Agamemnon and the Greek army just to get even with Agamemnon for his treachery.

"I have to admit," said Zeus, "there is no love lost between Agamemnon and myself, and I am already on the side of the Trojans in this war. But, while I am concerned about this earthly war, problems in the heavens need my attention. Right now a battle is raging among the gods on Olympus. Hera and you have been fighting on the side of the Greeks, while Apollo and Aphrodite are backing the Trojans. Nothing seems in order on Mount Olympus. The gods fight amongst themselves all the time."

To understand one of the reasons behind this discord, one must look back over a number of years. At the time, Zeus had selected Paris to judge a beauty contest between the goddesses Hera and Aphrodite. Son of the king of Troy, Paris was a handsome young man, but he was not especially smart. A year earlier, his father had ordered Paris to leave the palace because a prophecy had declared that disaster would fall on Troy if he remained. Paris was sent into the country-side to work as a shepherd—an exile that did not please him.

It was while he was struggling with his exile from the palace that Hera appeared to him. Telling him of the beauty contest he was to judge, she tried to boost her chances of winning by promising Paris that he could rule Europe and Asia if she were declared the victor.

"I will make you a courageous warrior who will lead the Trojan army to victory over the Greeks," declared Hera.

To counter Hera's offer, the goddess Aphrodite came to see Paris.

"If I am selected as the most beautiful," she said, I will give you a woman of incomparable beauty."

Aphrodite's offer was the one that most appealed to Paris.

At the time, Helen of Troy was considered the most beautiful woman in the world. Helen was said to be the natural daughter of Zeus, but she was raised by a king who insisted that she should only marry a powerful man. All of Helen's suitors were made to take a solemn oath that they would uphold the honor of any man that the king selected for her. This pledge, Helen's stepfather hoped, would prevent any rejected suitor from starting a war with Helen's new husband.

Of all who enthusiastically pursued the lovely Helen, it was Menelaus, the King of Sparta and a brother of Agamemnon, who won her. Her stepfather chose Menelaus to be Helen's husband. Unfortunately for Helen, Menelaus was much older than she was and not very handsome. The aging, unattractive Menelaus, though, could not have been happier with the prize he had won. His happiness was not to last.

"Helen is the woman I had in mind for Paris," Aphrodite pouted. "She is doubtless the most beautiful woman alive and she is much too good for Menelaus. I will keep my promise. I won the beauty contest, and now Paris shall have his reward." So eager was Aphrodite to fulfill her part of the deal that it did not matter to her that Helen was now married.

To put her plan in motion, Aphrodite sent Paris to Sparta, where King Menelaus graciously received the young prince. Soon after Paris' arrival, Aphrodite contrived things so that Menelaus was called away on official business. He was scarcely out of sight when Paris and Helen, who fell in love as soon as their eyes met, fled the palace and sailed for Troy.

When he heard the news of his wife's betrayal, Menelaus was heartbroken.

"I'll find Paris and bring my beloved Helen home, for I cannot live without her grace and beauty. I will do anything necessary to get my Helen back," moaned the lovesick King to his brother Agamemnon. Agamemnon quickly pledged his support, and thus began the war between Greece and Troy.

Shortly after the Greeks decided to go to

war, Menelaus approached Odysseus and asked him to honor a previous obligation and join the Greeks in what was to be a ten-year war. But the wily Odysseus, not wanting to leave the comforts of his palace to suffer and risk his life on the battlefield, feigned madness.

Menelaus closely watched Odysseus toss salt instead of seeds into the furrowed earth he was plowing.

"While I'm almost positive that Odysseus is only pretending, I'll put him to the test to make sure," thought Menelaus, and he pushed Odysseus' young son into the path of the plow. When Odysseus halted the plow to avoid killing his son, Menelaus was convinced that insanity was no longer a good excuse for Odysseus not to go to war.

Achilles, too, tried to avoid joining the war. Warned by his mother of Menelaus' approach, Achilles dressed as a woman and went to another of his palaces. Although the servants told Menelaus that Achilles had vanished, Menelaus was not that easily put off, and sent Odysseus to search for Achilles. The Grecian army was determined to have every one of its heroes in camp.

As it turned out, nabbing Achilles was not a difficult task even though he had assumed the disguise of a woman. Odysseus walked into the palace in which he suspected Achilles was hiding. Unrolling a pack he carried, Odysseus said, "Here, ladies, is an exquisite ruby bracelet. And please, take a look at these diamond earrings." The women were awed by the fabulous jewelry Odysseus had brought as bait. The plan was working; all the women gathered around him.

Odysseus, who also had some fine-looking weapons with him, showed them to the women, but there was only one woman who showed an interest in these masculine weapons.

"So, you like swords and daggers, Madame Achilles. Come on; the game is over. Let's get involved in a real game—the game of war." Odysseus could not help but laugh at Achilles' ridiculous scheme.

The night before he was to leave, Achilles' mother appeared before him. "Son," said Athena, "I can promise you a short and glorious life, or a long but boring life. Which do you choose?"

"Mother," said Achilles, "why can I not have the best of both?"

"It is so ordained that you may have only one or the other," she replied.

"In that case," said Achilles, "I choose the short but glorious life."

"Come then," she said, as she led him to the river Styx. There she grabbed him by the heel and dipped him into the river. As a result, neither arrows, nor swords, nor any other manmade weapons could hurt him. The heel by which Athena had held him was his only vulnerable spot.

With all of the key warriors in place, the war began. The fighting was merciless on both sides, and significant loss of life from battle, disease, and destruction came to both armies. Because of the misery that war brought, there was rising discontent in the Trojan camp. On the streets, Trojans could be heard saying, "We're sick of protecting Helen and living with all of this misery. Send her back! Send her back to Menelaus and Greece!

Send her back and stop the war!"

Zeus, feeling pity for both sides, did his best to help the warring countries end the war, but whenever he got things settled down, the goddesses Hera or Athena stepped in and sparked off some problem that started the fighting anew.

Once Paris and Menelaus engaged in man-to-man combat with spears. As the tide of battle swept back and forth, Menelaus threw a spear that sailed straight at Paris' chest. Aphrodite, however, broke the weapon while it was in flight.

"I will fight you bare-handed," shouted the determined Menelaus. Then, leaping upon Paris' back, he grabbed hold of the younger man's helmet. He was dragging him toward the Greek camp when Aphrodite again appeared.

"O, no! You will not harm a single hair on his head. Come, my darling," said Aphrodite as she swooped down and released the strap of Paris' helmet. Menelaus was left holding a helmet in his hand, and Paris had disappeared. While the confused Menelaus stood there, Aphrodite carried Paris back to Troy.

"Where is he? Paris must be somewhere close," swore an angry Menelaus as he searched the battlefield. Unable to locate Paris, Menelaus declared himself victorious and, as the victor in their one-on-one fight, Menelaus demanded that Helen be returned to him. The Trojan War appeared to have come to an end until a Trojan officer shot an arrow at Menelaus. This single arrow was enough to rekindle the bloody conflict.

Once again, the war raged, and shortly a heated battle took place between Diomedes and the Trojan prince, Aeneas. Diomedes, though he lacked the greatness of Achilles, was a highly respected warrior. Because of the fame of the combatants, there was such interest in the fight that the Trojan army stood along the walls of Troy to watch the two men. At one point, Aeneas, Aphrodite's son, was in grave danger of being killed, when the goddess swooped down and rescued him. When she did so, Diomedes struck Aphrodite, causing a slight wound to her hand. Aphrodite, losing her grip, let Aeneas plunge to the ground; it was only through Apollo's intervention that Aeneas was saved from death.

Aphrodite's interference so angered Zeus that he said, "Aphrodite, can't you stay out of trouble? I'm telling you for the last time to stay away from the battlefield."

Thus scolded, Aphrodite did stay away, and Diomedes piled up a long list of victories.

Diomedes now felt ready to challenge the greatest of the Trojan warriors, Hector. Hector, the oldest son of King Priam of Troy, was the heir to the throne of Troy and had distinguished himself with bravery, courage, and skill throughout the long war. As he walked toward the battlefield to seek out Hector, Diomedes muttered to himself, "Who stands behind my opponent? Is it the war god Ares who protects Hector?" Assuming that the god of war was on Hector's side, Diomedes was deeply troubled.

While it is true that the war god was on the battlefield, he was not much of a help to Hector. "Ares might be my son," said Hera, "but he is not brave. He would run like a hunted rabbit if an arrow came within a mile of him. He might appear to be brave, but I know better." She then took the side of Diomedes and encouraged him to fight. Athena, who also secretly joined in on Diomedes' side, encouraged him to use his bow. When Diomedes let his arrow fly, the arrow hit Ares, causing him much more pain than even Athena had expected.

Bawling and screaming, Ares flew to the safety of Mt. Olympus, where he complained to Zeus about his treatment at the hands of Athena.

"Keep away from battlefields, and you won't get hurt," advised Zeus, who could not stop laughing at the cowardly Ares.

Back on the battlefield, the fighting was thunderous and bloody, and at one point the Trojans nearly wiped out Agamemnon and his army. This beating almost forced Agamemnon to withdraw his troops and return to Greece, but Hera decided to take action.

"You, Zeus, my dear husband," she said, "are wonderful. You are a truly thoughtful, caring husband, but, my hardworking love, you need to relax. Here, rest your head on my lap. Let me run my fingers through your hair and soothe you to sleep."

Hera swiftly locked Zeus into a deep sleep. With Zeus unconscious, Hera was able to do as she liked, and Hera, once again, aided the Greeks in their battles.

When Zeus finally awoke, he was furious. He searched out Hera and began to shout at her. "I'm innocent," Hera lied. "I had nothing to do with the Greeks' impressive victories."

These victories, at any rate, were short-lived. Zeus immediately gave assistance to the Trojans, and his assistance helped turned the tide of the war in their favor.

Achilles turned over his armor to his best friend, Patroclus. For Patroclus, it was a great honor to be allowed to replace Achilles on the battlefield. Wearing the great hero's magnificent armor made Patroclus' heart swell with pride and he eagerly went off to fight with the Greek army.

Soon afterwards, Achilles received the news that Patroclus had been killed by Hector. Achilles was left numb with pain and grief. He had lost the one person who meant the most to him. "Hector will die for this. He will die by my hands," swore Achilles.

Hearing Achilles' vow, Athena appeared. She understood that Achilles' grief over Patroclus' death counted for more than his anger at Agamemnon, and she said to him, "Here, wear this armor I had made for you. It was made by the great blacksmith himself, Hephaestus. Achilles, this suit will protect you from the stab of all swords and spears. Go and do what you must to avenge your dead friend."

"Until Patroclus' death has been avenged, I will not have food nor drink," Achilles vowed, and he left to join Agamemnon and the other troops. As Achilles approached the battlefield, he saw that both armies had already lined the walls surrounding Troy in anticipation of this important fight. He and Hector walked toward each other from opposite sides of the field; all eyes were on the two famous warriors. The two stood with weapons in their hands. The air was electrified. The mother of all battles began, and poor Hector did not know that Achilles was doubly protected by Athena. After striking Achilles several times and causing no wounds, Hector said, "What is happening? No matter where I strike Achilles, my sword draws no blood."

At that very moment, Achilles knocked Hector's sword from his hand. Defenseless without a weapon, Hector ran, and Achilles chased after him. Around the walled city of Troy they ran until finally, Achilles caught Hector. They fought, but for Hector there was little chance. Achilles plunged his sword into his opponent's chest, and Hector fell dead.

"Here's Hector, your Trojan hero," Achilles shouted to the army of Troy. "He doesn't look so brave now that he is only a corpse dragged around by my chariot. People of Troy, I give you your hero, Hector!" Achilles shouted. Even dragging the body of Hector around the city, however, was not enough to cool the rage inside Achilles. When asked by Hector's family to return the body so a proper burial could take place, Achilles would not agree to do so. Zeus intervened and made sure that Hector, whom he cared for, received an honorable burial. It was not long after this incident that Achilles met

his own death. Some say it was Paris who let fly the arrow that hit Achilles in his one unprotected spot, the heel that had not been dipped in the river Styx. Others claim that it was the god Apollo, in the form of Paris, who actually shot the arrow that killed the great Greek hero The war dragged on nevertheless, and it became clear that the stubborn and war-weary armies were at a standoff. For the soldiers, there appeared little reason for continuing the fight. By this point, Paris was dead and Helen's whereabouts were unknown. Few soldiers were even clear as to why the war was being fought. It continued nonetheless.

"We must do something to achieve a final victory," said Odysseus. "We must get inside Troy." Addressing a group of high-ranking officers, he said, "We will have a fake horse built. It should be large enough to hide many men inside. We will hide some of our best soldiers within the horse. Then, the rest of the army will pack up their gear and board our ships and appear to sail away. The Trojans who come and examine the horse will think it is an offering of ours to the gods, and they will pull it inside the city of Troy to

convert it to their own use. Once inside the city walls, our soldiers will sneak out of the horse at night, kill the guards, and open the gates of the fortress. Silently, our entire army will come out of hiding and overrun the sleeping city of Troy."

Agamemnon and all the others agreed that it was worth a try.

As planned, the army started packing up its equipment, boarding ships, and acting as though preparing to set sail. The idea was to pretend to give up the siege of Troy, and it worked perfectly. The Trojans who watched from the walls of their city were overjoyed. They were also astounded by the large wooden horse that the Greeks had left on the shore. After the Greeks had left, the Trojans did as Odysseus had predicted and brought the horse inside the city walls.

"I do not trust that wooden horse," said a suspicious priest. "There is more here than we know," he warned. Ignoring his warnings, a large crowd gathered around the great wooden horse.

From high above the city, Athena watched the priest talking against the wooden horse. Annoyed at the thought that he might spoil Odysseus plan, Athena released two huge snakes from her temple and sent them to earth. The snakes immediately sought out and killed the priest and his two sons.

For the rest of the day, victory celebrations were held all over Troy. Then, late that night, when all was quiet, the Greek soldiers hiding inside the wooden horse crept out, overpowered the guards at the city's gates, and let in the rest of the Greek army that had only appeared to sail away. Exhausted from their celebrations, the Trojans were easy prey. The Greek army easily defeated the soldiers of Troy.

When Troy was captured, some Trojans were more fortunate than others. Aeneas, although rescued by his mother Aphrodite, lost his wife and children in the raid. Aphrodite assisted in the rescue of Helen, and returned her to Menelaus. Because Menelaus was ecstatic to have his wife returned, he forgave her treacherous betrayal.

As was the custom, the Trojan women and children were carried off as slaves by the Greeks. In a final act of vengeance, the Greeks, just before they left, burned the city of Troy. Houses were put to the torch, and Troy was left in ruins. The Trojan War had finally come to an end. ✿

Odysseus' Voyage Home

WITH THE WAR ended, Odysseus left Troy to return to Ithaca, where the wife and son that he hadn't seen for ten years were waiting. With twelve ships and one hundred and fifty men, Odysseus began the long journey home. Little did he realize as he sailed from the shores of Troy that it would be another ten years before he would finally see home. It was written by the gods that Odysseus would arrive home only after many misadventures.

The first stop he and his crew made was at an island called the Land of the Ciconians. There the inhabitants attacked Odysseus and his crew, killing seventy-two of his men. Nine days later in the land of the Lotus Eaters, some of his men unwittingly ate flowers containing a drug. This drug made the men unwilling to leave the island, and they had to be tied up and dragged back aboard the ship.

One of the worst trials Odysseus and his crew experienced was an encounter with the one-eyed monster Polyphemus, who belonged to the race called Cyclopes. Polyphemus gazed greedily as Odysseus and some of his crew left their ship to come ashore and forage for food. With the single red eye in the center of his forehead, the Cyclops watched as the men looked for wild game. He knew they would also look for a spring with fresh water and some fruit to replenish their supplies. As the men, unaware they were being watched, made their way up a hill, Polyphemus eagerly licked his lips. He planned to have several of them for his next meal.

After a short time, Odysseus and twelve of his men reached the top of the hill. They saw a cave and went to investigate. This cave was Polyphemus' home.

From his hiding place, the Cyclops watched as Odysseus and his men walked into the cave. When the men were inside, the giant, never blinking his single eye, rolled a huge stone over the entrance. Later that day, the Cyclops returned home and picked two of the trapped men and ate them for his supper.

"That was certainly tasty, but now I'm tired. It's been a hard day for me," muttered Polyphemus sleepily. Soon, the monster had fallen fast asleep.

Meanwhile, Odysseus gathered his ten remaining men in a corner of the cave.

"We've got to get out of here," Odysseus told them, "but we'll wait until morning. I will come up with some plan by then." As the men returned to sit in a corner of the cave, all were trembling with fear.

When morning arrived, Polyphemus approached the frightened cluster of men, and he grabbed two more for his breakfast. "I'll be back for lunch. Stand a little closer to the fire; I like my meat slightly roasted." He left them with a maniacal laugh trailing after him.

"Our swords are of no use against that creature. It would be like sticking him with a pin," cried one of the terrified men.

"Perhaps," said another, "if we used all of our swords to jab him at once, it would do some harm."

"No," said Odysseus, "he would just take away our swords. Here is what I have been thinking. First, we will use our swords to carve a point on a large piece of wood. That one over there near the fire will do; it's as big as a small tree. When the monster falls asleep tonight, we will sharpen the stick to a fine point. Then, we will heat the end of the log in the burning hearth. When the tip is red hot, we will plunge it into the eye of the sleeping monster."

All of the men agreed, although each man knew that two of them would no longer be there after the monster had his dinner.

Later that day, the giant returned to his cave and ate two more of Odysseus' men. Polyphemus, having eaten, again decided to take a nap. Immediately, Odysseus and his men put their plan in motion. The wooden stake, having already been sharpened, was placed in the fire and, when it was ready, they plunged it into the monster's eye.

The Cyclops screamed and jumped up. "Arghh! Ahh! I . . . I can't see!" In his panic, the Cyclops rolled aside the boulder and rushed out of the cave. Then, remembering his prisoners and fearing they might escape, he began feeling around on the ground for his captives. Odysseus and his men, however, were still inside the cave. While Polyphemus was screaming and shouting, they had hidden themselves underneath the bodies of the small flock of giant sheep that Polyphemus kept in the cave. The men reasoned that, while the creature would never let them out, he would need to put his sheep out to graze.

"Hold on, men. Hang on to the sheep's bellies, and we'll get out of here," Odysseus whispered.

As Odysseus had predicted, Polyphemus let the sheep pass out of the cave without ever thinking to inspect their undersides. Once Odysseus and his men were safely out of the cave, Odysseus began to taunt the monster. In a rage, the Cyclops shouted, "Who are you? Who put out my eye? What is your name?"

Odysseus answered, "My name is No Man!" Then, fearing Polyphemus' screams and shouts might attract other Cyclopes, Odysseus and his men quickly made their way to their boat. As they set sail, Polyphemus' neighbors did arrive at his cave.

"What is wrong?" they asked. "Who did this to you?"

But all the Cyclops could answer was, "No Man did this to me." Once they heard this answer, all that the Cyclops' neighbors could do was stand there and shrug their shoulders.

After the thinned-out crew escaped from Polyphemus, Odysseus encountered the Sirens, women who sat on rocks along the ocean shore and sang beautiful songs. They had caused hundreds of shipwrecks by luring the sailors and ships on to the rocks with enchanted songs. Odysseus prevented his men from wrecking there by putting wax in their ears so they could not hear the Sirens' seductive songs. Curious to hear them himself, he did not plug up his own ears, but had his men tie him tightly to the ship's mast. When he heard the Sirens sing, Odysseus was filled with the same yearning that had destroyed so many other men and struggled to loosen his bonds, but he could not. He had told his crew not to free him no matter how much he pleaded. The ship passed by the Sirens unharmed.

While there were other dangers along the way, the worst occurred as Odysseus and his men were nearing the end of their journey.

Many years earlier, a beautiful witch named Circe had promised Odysseus that he and his men would have a safe journey, as Odysseus had softened her heart. Unlike many men, Odysseus had not been captivated by Circe's bewitching beauty. Circe was not aware that Athena had given him an herb that made him immune to Circe's spells. Odysseus' powers of resistance amazed the lovely sorceress, and the fact that she couldn't have him made him all the more desirable a prize.

As Odysseus and his men approached the land of the sun, Circe, speaking through an ancient priest, gave them a warning.

"You must not fool with or touch the golden oxen of the sun. You are sure to see them at some point along the way, but you must not, I repeat, must not disturb those oxen"

"Odysseus," Circe continued, "I can predict with confidence that you will have a safe passage home; unfortunately, I cannot say the same for your crew."

Odysseus thanked Circe for the warning and doubled the men on watch. Shortly afterwards they spotted an island. Landing on the shore, some went in search of food and water. The search party came upon some fat oxen grazing on the island. Forgetting Circe's warning, the hungry men killed the beasts and ate them. That evening as they sailed from the island, a storm came in. As Circe had predicted, a thunderbolt hit their ship and all the men drowned. Only Odysseus was able to cling to the side of the ship and ride out the raging storm.

In the meantime at his home in Ithaca, Odysseus' wife Penelope and son Telemachus lived for the day that Odysseus would return. During his absence of close to twenty years, Penelope and Telemachus had been living under unbearable conditions. Hordes of men, seeking to take the queen as a wife and gain the riches of the palace, invaded their home. These invaders made life for the mother and son a constant misery. The ill-mannered suitors were having a merry time in the palace. As they drank the fine wines and feasted on the rich food, drunken brawls were commonplace. Penelope, who was a devoted wife, prayed constantly for Odysseus' return to Ithaca.

"Telemachus, I want nothing to do with these ill-mannered men. I will wait forever if that is what it takes for your father to return," said Penelope sadly.

"Each one of those ruthless, ill-mannered men thinks he is the one who is going to convince you to marry him. It's laughable," remarked Telemachus.

"But," Penelope said, "this place is getting too dangerous for you now that you are older. Until I can figure a way to rid the palace of these men, I must send you away. It is for your own good. Because they resent you, your life is in danger. You are so like your father, so decent and kind." Penelope thought of Odysseus, and her eyes filled with tears. "I am sending you to Sparta, where you will be safe."

Telemachus, agreeing to his mother's wishes, told her that he had noticed the suitors' sly, evil glances and had overheard their remarks. "They clearly mean to harm me."

At the same time, unbeknownst to his loved ones, Odysseus, after twenty years and countless hardships, was finally returning to the shores of Ithaca and his family. As Odysseus prepared to land, Athena appeared to him.

"You will be murdered on the spot by your wife's suitors, Odysseus. You must keep them from recognizing you." This said, she swiftly changed Odysseus' appearance to that of a beggar. Then she led him to a cave where one of his devoted old servants lived. Guiding Telemachus to the same cave, Athena reunited the father and son.

As Odysseus walked into the cave, neither the servant Eumaeus nor Telemachus recognized him. Nevertheless, being a generous person, the old man showed the beggar kindness. Shortly, Athena nudged the servant Eumaeus out of the cave, and Odysseus was left alone with Telemachus.

After revealing his true identify to his son, Odysseus said, "Telemachus, my son, how happy I am. I have waited so long for this day. Believe me, many times I was saddened by the thought that I would never see you and my beloved Penelope again." The father and son embraced, weeping with joy.

After all of Telemachus' doubts were put to rest, he asked, "What shall we do? What can we do about those men who have invaded our home?"

"Tonight we will go to the palace," Odysseus said. "I will remain in disguise. When the fools are in a drunken stupor, you and I will hide all of their weapons, keeping two handy for our own use. Then we will take our revenge."

When Odysseus entered the palace that night, his ailing old dog recognized him immediately.

"If only I could pet him," Odysseus sadly thought. He knew that such an action would arouse the suitors' suspicions. The dog perked up long enough to look at Odysseus, sighed deeply, and died. It was as if the dog had waited all those years for the sight of his master and, that accomplished, was able to breathe his last breath. Odysseus could not hold back a soft, sorrowful moan.

"Hey, pass the wine and some more of that meat. Hurry it up! Stop hogging the food," shouted one of the men at the dining room table. At this point it was crowded with loud, drunken suitors.

"Hey, men, what do we have here? A beggar among us?" The rest of the suitors joined in and made fun of Odysseus.

"I think it is about time Penelope made up her mind," said another of the men. "Who of us is going to be the next king of Ithaca? Let us force her to make a choice."

"Yes. I'm tired of waiting around here. Let's do as you say," agreed another. With this suggestion, all in the room shouted agreement.

Still in the disguise of a beggar, Odysseus walked closer to Penelope. He listened as she poured out her heart. "O, how I miss him! I love Odysseus with all of my heart and soul. I shall never give in to these scoundrels." Odysseus' disguise had completely fooled Penelope as well as the suitors. She had no idea who this beggar was, but an old servant woman who came by at that moment stared at Odysseus' foot. She went up to the beggar and whispered in his ear.

"You are Odysseus. I would know you anywhere by the scar on your foot," said the old woman, who had tended to Odysseus when he was a child. The old nursemaid was bubbled with joy. "You got that old scar from a wound you received in a hunting accident when you were a lad of seven. I am so delighted to see you, dear boy."

Knowing he could trust her, Odysseus pulled her aside and said, "You must be careful not to reveal my identity."

In the meantime, Penelope, still not aware that Odysseus had returned, knew she had to stall for time. She said, "Since I am being forced to choose one of you, I will challenge you to a game of skill to determine which one. The man who can string Odysseus' bow and shoot an arrow through the rings hanging from the ceiling will be my next husband." She expected that none of the suitors would be able to perform this difficult feat, because, although many had tried, Odysseus was the only person who had ever been able to do it. Indeed, many of the suitors were not even able to string the bow or pull it taut, let alone shoot an arrow through the rings. I

It wasn't long until each suitor had tried and failed. At this point Odysseus stepped forward. The frustrated suitors watched scornfully as the beggar picked up the bow and an arrow.

"Well, look at this! A beggar is going to try to shoot arrows through the rings. Ha! He can't even put his pants on straight," yelled one of the suitors.

"If he has a decent pair of pants to put on," laughed another.

As they laughed, Odysseus, using all of his strength, pulled back the bow and let the arrow fly. Of course, it headed straight through the center of the rings.

"By the gods, what's going on here? Is this some kind of trick?" All of the suitors were skeptical, but, having no means of explaining what the trickery could be, they let it pass. They had no intentions, anyway, of letting this beggar marry the queen. They forgot the beggar's success for the moment and resumed their merrymaking, and by nightfall, all were drunk.

At this point, drunk and angry, a few suitors began to talk about the outcome of the shooting contest. As they spoke, they became more suspicious, and as their suspicions increased, they began reaching for their weapons. They were completely unaware that all their weapons had been removed by Odysseus and Telemachus.

In the doorway, Odysseus and Telemachus appeared. With few words they unleashed their attack. "Here, father, take this one," Telemachus said, handing his father one arrow after another. As quickly as he received them, Odysseus shot the arrows at the suitors. Soon, every one of the invaders lay dead upon the palace floor.

Penelope immediately realized who the archer was. In truth, when the beggar had shot the arrow through the rings, she had begun to suspect his identity. Now, with her hopes confirmed, she was openly joyful. Odysseus was back, and happiness could once again reign in Ithaca. ❀

Voyage of Odysseus

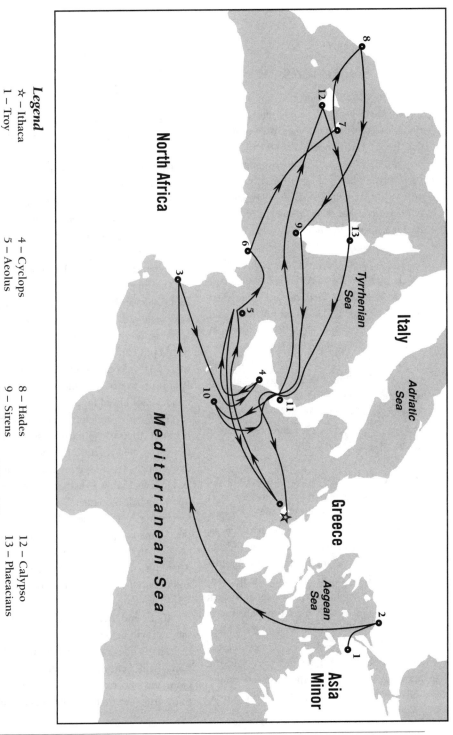

Legend
☆ – Ithaca
1 – Troy
2 – Cicones
3 – Lotus Eaters
4 – Cyclops
5 – Aeolus
6 – Laestryonians
7 – Circe
8 – Hades
9 – Sirens
10 – Scylla and Charybdis
11 – Helios
12 – Calypso
13 – Phaeacians

Aeneas

Aeneas, the mortal son of Venus, was one of the only surviving warriors after the fall of Troy. He sailed and wandered around the world much as Odysseus had. Aeneas' journey was described in The Aeneid, an epic written by the Roman poet, Virgil, who lived approximately 700-800 years after The Iliad and The Odyssey were written. Note that the gods are called by their Roman names in this tale.

A WOMAN NAMED DIDO founded the ancient city in Africa called Carthage, and under her rule, it flourished. Aeneas, a widower, landed in Carthage, and, as the gods arranged, Dido fell in love with him. He, however, soon wanted to leave.

"You must not leave me, Aeneas, I beg you," pleaded Queen Dido. "Stay in Carthage with me, and all that I have will be yours. This kingdom will be my dowry; its treasures will be your treasures. If I can't have you in my life, I don't care to live. Tell me that you will stay."

With these soft words, Queen Dido did everything she could to persuade her lover not to leave the country she ruled. Despite Dido's pleas and his own love for her, Aeneas, the hero warrior, was bound by a code of honor and the desires of the gods. Jupiter, king of gods and men, had sent the messenger god Mercury to Carthage. Mercury's task was to remind Aeneas to continue his travels and complete the mission of setting the stage for the founding of Rome. Aeneas obeyed, and on the day that he left Carthage, the heartsick Dido climbed upon a burial mound and stabbed herself. Lighting the burial mound, she set herself ablaze.

Far out at sea, the god Neptune guided Aeneas to his next adventure. As he set his course that night by the stars, Aeneas could not have guessed the tragic events the gods had in store for him.

High above Aeneas, a conversation about him was taking place.

"A life must be sacrificed if I am forced to permit Aeneas to reach Italy," insisted Neptune. He issued the demand to Venus, the goddess of love.

"What must be, must be," said Venus.

That night, while Palinurus, Aeneas' best friend, was at the ship's helm, Neptune called the sleep god Somnus to him. He directed Somnus to put a spell on Palinurus that would put Palinurus into a deep sleep. When this was accomplished, Somnus shoved Palinurus overboard where raging currents quickly swallowed him.

"How could something like this happen to my best friend? Palinurus was the person dearest to me," a grieving Aeneas said. "One day, though, I shall see my friend again, just as surely as I know I shall once again lay eyes upon my beloved father."

Having heard Aeneas' lament, a Sibyl— the Roman equivalent of a soothsayer— spoke with the god Apollo on Aeneas' behalf. After this, the Sibyl appeared before Aeneas and reported to him that more troubles, hardships, and dangers lay ahead.

"In the end, Aeneas, you will overcome all this and will be rewarded."

"Thank you, sweet Sibyl, for this information," said Aeneas. "I wonder if you might grant me one request. More than anything else, I desire to see my father, who is in the underworld where the dead reside. Can you help me?" asked Aeneas.

The Sibyl replied, "It is easy enough to go down to the underworld, Aeneas, but returning to the world again may prove to be difficult." The prophetess then told Aeneas that to accomplish the task, he must take a golden bough from a certain tree. "You are to give this golden bough to Persephone, Pluto's wife, as a gift."

Aeneas secured a golden bough, and, with the Sibyl to accompany him, he went down to the underworld. As they approached, they were met by a guide. The Sibyl introduced Aeneas and explained his purpose. Quite agreeably, the guide said, "This way, Aeneas. This passageway will take us to where it is you need to go." The guide set out, and Aeneas followed. As they walked, Aeneas became filled with terror because the place was inhabited by many frightful forms and figures. In speechless amazement, he saw Death, Hunger, and Fear. Walking further, he saw the Furies, those terrible female spirits that punish unavenged crimes. Then Aeneas passed close to the hissing nine-headed snake, the Hydra, and the fire-breathing monster, Chimera.

Coming to the river Styx, they met the ferryman Charon.

"Come!" Charon ordered, "I will ferry you across the Styx." Within minutes, Aeneas and the Sibyl had reached the opposite bank. When they left Charon's boat, they received an unfriendly greeting from Cerberus, the three-headed guard dog. But the Sibyl, prepared for this, tossed something to the growling monster. In seconds the creature's body slumped, and all three heads nodded in sleep.

Upon arriving at the center of the underworld, Aeneas said, "Ah! Just look at them! There are my old shipmates—and so many other people I once knew. How sad this makes me. Look there…over there; it's Dido. Dido, will you ever forgive me for leaving you?"

Seeing Dido was particularly shattering for Aeneas. When she did not respond, he cried mournfully, "Doesn't she hear me?" As an answer, the Sibyl reminded him that they were walking among the dead. To the dead, she said, words were unimportant; they spoke or answered as they pleased.

To Aeneas' surprise, a form appeared at his side. It was the recently deceased Palinurus. He begged, "Aeneas, please get me out of here. Carry me back to the outside world." While the pleas of his best friend touched Aeneas deeply, Aeneas was helpless. He could do nothing to aid his friend, and walked away from him with a heavy heart.

They soon reached a place called the Elysian Fields, which is where they found Anchises, Aeneas' father. Upon seeing his son, Anchises explained, "There are many Trojan statesmen and heroes here. All of them call on you to carry on their name in a glorious Roman nation. You, my son, must continue on your journey. In the end, you will be the founder of a great Roman state. This Roman nation you start will be more powerful than all of Greece and Troy combined."

The spirit of Aeneas' father departed, and Aeneas and the Sibyl began their journey home. Back on earth, Aeneas thanked the Sibyl for having taken him to the underworld and given him the opportunity to see his father and Palinurus. Then he set sail, and he and his men traveled along the coast of Italy.

Shortly, they arrived at the mouth of the Tiber River, at the land of Latium, where King Latinus ruled. King Latinus was a descendant of Saturn, god of agriculture. While Latinus had no sons, he did have a daughter, Lavinia, who was the most beautiful of women.

"Lavinia is pledged to wed Turnus, the King of the Rutulians," Latinus said, "but in you, Aeneas, I see a greater match for my beautiful daughter." When she heard her father say this, Lavinia smiled, for although she had told no one, she had been having dreams about a handsome Trojan. This Trojan, she dreamed, would be better looking, wiser, and kinder than any man she had ever known. Surely, she thought, this Aeneas must be the man of whom she had been dreaming.

Just as Lavinia had dreamed, she and Aeneas fell immediately in love. No doubt, a wedding would have followed quickly, but Juno, Queen of the Roman gods, interfered. Juno, who did not like the Trojans, stirred up conflict between Aeneas and King Turnus. In fact, Juno set off such a rivalry between the two men that war broke out. While King Turnus had the support of the warrior Camilla and many others, Aeneas was able to gain the assistance of the Etruscans. The neighbors of Latium, the Etruscans were a warlike people who had little love for Turnus. This hatred put Aeneas' army on equal standing with the king of the Rutulians.

The tide of battle, shifting back and forth all day, first favored Aeneas, then King Turnus. At one point, Aeneas slew two of the Rutulians' mightiest warriors, Mezentius and his son Lausus. Then Turnus killed Pellas, the son of King Evander and a good friend to Aeneas. Toward the end of the first day, a tired and discouraged Aeneas began to feel his spirit slip away. To rally him, Jupiter sent the three Fates to Aeneas' side. The Fates, who controlled human destiny and life, said, "Aeneas, we are here to protect you. Go into battle knowing that our protection goes with you." At the same time, the gods who would have liked to come to Turnus' aid were forbidden to do so by Jupiter. It was in this manner that the great conflict was decided in favor of Aeneas.

Turnus pleaded for his life after being knocked to the ground by Aeneas.

"Please do not kill me, Aeneas. Have mercy," begged Turnus. Aeneas, a man of great pity, was ready to shoulder his spear and spare Turnus' life, but at that moment a medal belonging to Pellas fell from Turnus' belt. Seeing Pellas' medal erased all the pity Aeneas had felt and filled him with rage.

"Your rage made you take that medal from Pellas. Turnus, this is revenge for Pellas." Aeneas jabbed the spear into his enemy, instantly killing him.

As the gods had desired, the triumphant Aeneas founded the state of Rome. He and Lavinia married, and he named a city in Italy in her honor. The union of Lavinia and Aeneas eventually resulted in the birth of the great Julius Caesar and the mighty Roman nation, the mightiest the world had yet seen.

❀

Comprehension Check

1. Based on their behavior during the Trojan war, how do you suppose the Greeks viewed their gods? Does their view seem strange to you?

2. Does the frequent intervention of the gods in the affairs of men signify that the Greeks had a dim view of man's ability to control events in his life?

3. Considering some selections, particularly those of Achilles' slaying of Hector and of Odysseus' slaying of the suitors, how would you respond to someone who said that the Greeks were awfully lacking in their notion of fair play. By referring to the stories, attack or support that position.

4. In the sentence, "The councilman began to hector the mayor," consider the word "hector." State the meaning of the word, and identify its classical derivation.

CHAPTER 7

THE HOUSE OF ATHENS

Cecrops

ECROPS WAS THE first King of Attica, even though he was only partly human. During his reign, it is said that he was responsible for the goddess Athena becoming the protector of Athens. There was a time when both Poseidon and Athena wanted the city. To show how great a benefactor he could be, Poseidon created a well of salt water by striking the rock of the Acropolis with his trident. Not to be outdone, Athena made an olive tree—the most precious tree in all of Greece—grow there.

Cecrops was the mediator in this showdown and decided that, because of her gracious gift, Athens would belong to Athena. When Cecrops made his decision, Poseidon became incensed and sent a great flood to destroy Athens and punish its people.

In an alternate story, a vote took place to determine the winner of Athens. All of the women voted for Athena and all of the men voted for Poseidon. Since there was exactly one more woman than there were men, Athena won. When Poseidon flooded Athens, the male Greeks, in their anger, decreed that women could not vote.

Both tales agree on one point: it was in the family of Cecrops that the tragedies of the Athenian women began. 🌸

Procne and Philomela

PROCNE AND PHILOMELA, two sisters, were separated for many years. While they were separated, Procne, who was married to Tereus, a son of Athens, had a son. When Procne's son, Itys, turned five, Procne asked Tereus if she could invite her sister to visit. Tereus agreed but decided that he would go fetch Philomela from Athens himself.

When Tereus arrived in Athens to escort Philomela, he was amazed at Philomela's beauty. He instantly fell in love and wanted to have her as his own. He persuaded Philomela's father to let her go back with him. Philomela was flattered at Tereus' attention and excited to be making the voyage.

Tereus and Philomela's voyage was uneventful. They traveled well together, and Philomela was looking forward to seeing her sister. As the travelers disembarked and began their journey over land toward the palace, Tereus lied to Philomela and told her that he had received word that her sister had died. Philomela was distraught. She had not seen her sister for many years and was heartbroken that she would never be able to see her now. Taking advantage of Philomela's distress, Tereus persuaded her to marry him.

As Tereus and Philomela continued the journey, now as husband and wife, Philomela learned that Tereus had tricked her. In her anger, she threatened, "How dare you prey on my emotions and lie to me about my sister! No man will ever respect you now, after your despicable behavior. I will tell everyone how you have manipulated me for your own benefit!"

At her words, Tereus was angered and scared that she might be right. To save himself, Tereus cut out Philomela's tongue and left her heavily guarded. He continued his journey alone, preparing a story to tell Procne, who was anticipating her sister's arrival.

When Tereus arrived at the palace, he greeted Procne with reddened eyes and sadness in his voice. "My heart grieves at the news I bear, Procne. On our journey to meet you, your sister passed away." Procne was devastated. Because she had no way of knowing otherwise and because Tereus was so convincing, she mourned the loss of her sister.

Tereus thought to himself, "Now I have nothing to fear. Philomela will never be able to tell her story, and Procne has no reason to doubt the story I have told her."

Philomela believed all was hopeless. She was locked away under constant surveillance, and even if she were able to escape, she would have no means of communicating her story, for she could not write. As Philomela contemplated her case, she began to ponder the craftsmen who were able to tell stories through what they made with their hands. She thought about those who could depict hunting scenes and harvest scenes with amazing detail on shields. Likewise, women illustrated tales in the tapestries they wove. Inspired, Philomela turned to her loom. Her hands were like magic. With the greatest skill, Philomela wove a tapestry was so intricate that it was able to tell the whole story of what had happened to her at Tereus' hands. When the tapestry was complete, Philomela gave it to the old woman that came to tend her, and told her that the tapestry was a gift for the queen.

The old woman was delighted at the quality of the fine tapestry. She proudly took it to Procne, who was still greatly saddened by her sister's death. When Procne unrolled the tapestry, she was amazed to see Philomela staring back at her. With great sadness in her heart, Procne read what had happened to Philomela as it was illustrated in the details of the tapestry. With horror, she set her eyes upon her husband's face, suspended in the fibers woven with Philomela's fingers. Outraged, Procne meditated upon a just punishment for Tereus and a means of freeing her tormented sister.

Hiding her anger and pretending to want to thank the woman who had woven the tapestry personally, Procne asked the old woman to take her to Philomela. When Procne saw her sister, she began to weep. She told Philomela all that she had discovered and took her sister back to the palace. Philomela cried tears of happiness as she was reunited with her sister, and as Philomela wept, Procne swore, "I am prepared to do anything to make Tereus pay for the pain that he has caused you."

As Procne thought, anger boiled inside her. Unaware of the situation, Procne's son, Itys, came to see his mother. When Procne's gaze fell on Itys, she thought to herself, "You, my son, are so like your father and all of his detestable ways." As she spoke, the means of revenge became clear and, with no hesitation, Procne killed her own son with a swift thrust of her silver dagger. She cut the tiny body up and prepared the pieces to serve for Tereus' dinner that evening. As Tereus ate what he believed were pieces of beef, Procne watched him carefully. When he was finished with his meal, Procne divulged what he had been eating.

Tereus was horrified. At first, he could not even gain control of his legs enough to chase after his wife as she and Philomela made their escape. Then Tereus recovered and was able to run after them. Just as he was overtaking them, the gods turned the two sisters into birds so they could fly away. Procne was transformed into a nightingale, and Philomela was turned into a swallow. Because Procne would never forget the son she killed, the song of the nightingale is both beautiful and sad; Philomela's missing tongue is the reason the swallow is only capable of a dull chirp and never sings.

Finally, Tereus was also changed into a bird. The gods turned him into a hideous vulture. ✿

Procris and Cephalus

EVERY MORNING, a beautiful young man woke to hunt. Cephalus loved sports and would spend each morning in the forest. One morning, Aurora, the goddess of the dawn, caught sight of him. When Aurora first laid eyes on Cephalus, she immediately fell in love and decided that she must make this handsome youth her own.

Aurora approached Cephalus, her face suffused with adoration.

"Sweet youth, you embody all that is natural and beautiful. Come with me and we can spend every morning for eternity rising with the sun."

While Cephalus was flattered at the goddess' attentions, he had just married a woman whom he loved greatly: Procris, the niece of Philomela and Procne.

"Forgive me, goddess, but I have a glorious wife to whom I will be forever devoted."

"But I can give you daybreak for your hunting. I can illuminate the forest with golden sun so the dew glistens on the branches. What has this wife of yours ever given you?" Aurora countered.

"My wife is loved by Diana, the goddess of hunting. Diana gave Procris a dog that could outrun any rival and a javelin that would never miss its mark; my wife, in turn, gave these gifts to me," replied Cephalus.

Aurora was disappointed and angry.

"Ungrateful man! Go back to your unfaithful wife, but I warn you that, some day, you will regret your decision to stay with her. You will wish that you had never seen her again." With those words, Aurora vanished.

When Cephalus heard what Aurora had said, he was mad with jealousy. He had been away from home for so long, and his wife was extremely beautiful. How could he be sure that she had been faithful to him? Cephalus realized that he would never be at ease unless he could prove to himself that Procris loved only him. He resolved to disguise himself to see if Procris could be tempted by another man.

Expertly disguised, Cephalus returned home. He saw that his household was anxious for his return, but he did not reveal his true identity. When he saw Procris, though, her, he almost abandoned his plan. Procris was grief-stricken by her husband's absence. Tears streaked her face and her whole manner showed it. Nevertheless, Cephalus was intent on proving her fidelity.

Day after day, Cephalus tried to seduce Procris into falling in love with him, but, believing he was a stranger, Procris remained true to her "absent" husband. Even when the stranger continually told Procris that her husband had deserted her, Procris remained unswerved.

"I belong to only Cephalus," she said matter-of-factly. "My love for him is true,

regardless of where he is or what he does."

The time came, however, when Procris' resolve wore down. After countless petitions, persuasions, and promises, at one time, Procris did not immediately give the same response; instead, she hesitated. Cephalus believed her hesitation represented a denial of her love for him. "Terrible woman!" he raged. "The man you see before you is your husband. You have betrayed me with your lack of a response."

After his outburst, Procris simply looked at him, quietly got up, turned, and, without speaking, left. To have seen her dismissal of him, one would think that all of her love had turned to hate. She hated all men and went to live alone.

Cephalus was devastated by his loss. He realized the mistake that he had made in driving her away. Hunting high and low, he finally found her and begged her forgiveness. Procris was not to forgive Cephalus so easily; he was still very angry at his deception. Eventually, though, Cephalus won his way back into her heart.

Cephalus and Procris spent many joyous days together. One day, the two lovers went hunting together, as they often did. With them they took the javelin that Diana had given Procris, the one that never missed its target. When they reached the forest, both went off in search of game. Soon Cephalus perceived movement in the distance. Hoping to make the first kill, he threw the javelin. Like always, the javelin struck home. When Cephalus went to retrieve his prize, he found Procris lying on the ground, the javelin through her heart. ❁

Orithyia and Boreas

PROCRIS HAD A sister named Orithyia whom Boreas, the North Wind, deeply loved. All of Athens, and, more importantly, Orithyia's father, were against any marriage between the two. The people of Athens were prejudiced toward anyone who came from the North because of the sad fate that had come to Philomela and Procne. Athens refused to give the maiden Orithyia to Boreas to marry.

The people were mistaken in their refusal. Not only was their prejudice wrong-minded; it was also naïve to imagine that they would be able to stop the North Wind from getting what he wanted.

One day, when Orithyia was playing on the bank of a river with her sisters, Boreas swept down in a great gust and bore her away. ❁

Creüsa and Ion

PROCRIS AND ORITHYIA had another sister, Creüsa—and, like her sisters, Creüsa was also to suffer. One day, when she was a young girl, she was out gathering crocuses on a cliff, placing the flowers into her veil, which served as a makeshift basket. Noticing that her veil was full, Creüsa turned to go home. As she was leaving, Creüsa was grabbed by a man who seemed to appear out of nowhere. The man was beautiful, as perfect looking as a god, but Creüsa was so terrified that she did not notice his beauty. As he carried her off, Creüsa screamed in terror.

She did not realize that she was being kidnapped by Apollo himself. He carried Creüsa off to a cave near the cliff that was covered with yellow crocuses.

Time passed, and Creüsa became pregnant with Apollo's child. Apollo offered her no help, and she could not tell her parents what had happened, because she could be killed for having lost her virginity, even to a forceful god. Creüsa delivered a healthy baby boy, but, because she knew that she would have to explain his presence, she left him in the cave to die.

Creüsa tried to continue with her life, but her imagination was haunted by what might have happened to the son she abandoned. Unable to control her curiosity, she returned to the dark cave to see what fate had befallen her child. She found the cave empty, with no sign of her son remaining. There was no blood, so he couldn't have been eaten by wild animals. Creüsa looked for the veil and cloak that she had wrapped him in, but they were nowhere to be found. Terrible thoughts ran through Creüsa's head as she left the cave and trudged back home.

Some time later, Creüsa was married to a man that had helped her father, King Erechtheus, in a war. The foreigner, called Xuthus, was not from Athens, but he was a Greek. The Athenians viewed Xuthus as a stranger to their land, and while they approved of the marriage, they were not saddened when the young couple did not have any children. Xuthus was upset, because he wanted a son desperately. He and Creüsa went to Delphi and asked the Oracle if they had any hope of having a son.

Creüsa left Xuthus with one of the priests and traveled to the sanctuary on her own to ponder what had become of her life. When she reached the outer court, she found a beautiful young man dressed as a priest. He looked at her with such kindness that she returned his gaze. They began to talk and the youth told her, "I can tell by your manner that you are a woman of high standing. You appear to have lived a life that has been greatly blessed by the gods."

"Nonsense! My life has been nothing but misery and sorrow," Creüsa responded passionately. Looking at the wonder in the boy's eyes at her outburst, Creüsa quickly composed herself and asked him who he was.

"You are so young to be so dedicated as to serve one of Greece's holiest shrines. Where are you from?"

"My name is Ion. I am saddened to tell you that I do not know where I came from. When I was just a baby, Apollo's priestess and prophetess, the Pythoness, found me. She has raised me as a mother would. I cannot dream of a better way to spend my days than in serving the gods. But, my fair lady, why are you so sad? Your eyes are wet with tears. That is not how people come to Delphi; they rejoice as they come to the pure shrine of Apollo."

"I do not want to come near Apollo!" said Creüsa. Ion was startled by Creüsa's adamant answer and looked at her with anger. "I come in secret on an errand for a friend. My husband has come to Delphi to ask if he might hope for a son, but I come to discover the fate of another child who was the son of…" Creüsa faltered as she began to explain. Then she spoke again quickly, as if scared

that she would not reveal her purpose if she thought about what she was going to say. "…of a friend of mine. She is a sad woman whom this holy god of yours defiled. When this child was born, after Apollo forced her to bear it, she left the baby boy in a dark cave. My friend longs to know what has happened to this baby boy, and since it happened years ago, she longs to know how her baby died."

"This cannot be true," responded Ion, horrified that Creüsa should make such an accusation against the god. "Your friend tried to justify her shame by blaming the actions of a man on the god," he retorted hotly.

"No. I am sure that it was Apollo," Creusa said positively.

Ion was silent and said, "Even if you are right in your blame, you cannot approach Apollo to try to prove that he is guilty of such a despicable crime. You would be putting yourself in a terrible position."

"You are right," Creüsa spoke solemnly. "I will hold my tongue. " Creüsa was trying to understand her own feelings. As she and Ion were looking at each other, Xuthus entered the outer court and ran to where his wife was standing. Looking at Ion, Xuthus embraced the boy, who withdrew as if he were going to be touched by poison. "Apollo has said that you are my son!" cried Xuthus.

Immediately Creüsa spoke up with a sense of antagonism in her voice. "Your son?" she questioned. "If he is your son, who could his mother be?"

Xuthus was confused. "I don't know who his mother is, but Apollo told me he was my son."

The three stood there, all lost in their own

emotions. Xuthus was confused about what had taken place, but he was happy that he finally had a son. Ion was distant toward his new, unexpected parents, and Creüsa was overcome with anger. She felt nothing but hatred toward men and could not fathom mothering this child.

As the group was deep in thought, Apollo's prophetess entered, bringing with her two items: a veil and a maiden's cloak. To Xuthus, she said, "The priest must speak with you," and as she left, she handed Ion the veil and cloak. She looked directly at him and said, "Ion, when I found you, you were wrapped in these."

Ion was perplexed.

"My mother, whoever she was, must have left them with me. I can use this veil and cloak to find her. I will search the world using these clues."

Before Ion could think, Creüsa had rushed upon him with her arms open wide and called her son, her abandoned child.

Having already been confronted with life-changing news that day, Ion dismissed Creüsa, all the time believing that she was mad.

"My child," cried Creüsa, "the cloak and veil are what I wrapped you in when I left you. When I told you I was here to see Apollo for a friend of mine, I was protecting myself. It was not a friend who was concerned about the baby she left; it was me! Apollo truly is your father. Please believe me, Ion. I can prove what I am saying to you. Unfold the garments. Since I made them with my own hands, I know what is there. See if you can find the two serpents. I put them there. If these garments aren't mine, how do I know details about them?"

Ion inspected the garments, found the two little serpents, and turned to Creüsa with wonder in his eyes, "My mother, is Apollo my father? Did he lie in saying that I was Xuthus' son?"

"When Apollo spoke, he did not say that you were Xuthus' own son. Apollo gave you to Xuthus as a gift," Creüsa answered.

Instantly, a brilliant glow suffused the sky. Creüsa and Ion gazed up toward the heavens, struck by the beauty of the form that appeared before them.

Pallas Athena said, "Apollo has sent me to explain that Ion is both his son and yours. After you left him in the cave, Apollo had him brought to Delphi. He wants you to take Ion to Athens with you. Ion should rule there."

With those words, the vision departed and both Ion and Creüsa looked at each other and beamed.

The Danaïds

THE FIFTY YOUNG maidens known as the Danaïds were the descendants of the Nile-dwelling Io. These women, daughters of Danaüs, were cousins to the fifty sons of Danaüs' brother Aegyptus. Their cousins wished more than anything to marry the Danaïds, but the young maidens turned up their noses and ran away with their father.

After the Danaïds fled, they landed on the island of Argos, where the women were allowed to stay and were given sanctuary in case anyone should come to try to take them. Eventually, the sons of Aegyptus made their way to the island of Argos, intending to fight for their brides. Honoring their promise to the Danaïds, the residents turned the invaders away, because the Argives—as they were called—would not let a woman be forced to marry someone she did not want to marry.

At this point in the myth, there is an act change, as if in a play. The story resumes with the wedding of the Danaïds to the sons of Aegyptus, but it was not a wedding by choice. The Danaïds still did not want to marry their cousins. At the wedding feast, Danaüs gave each of his daughters a dagger, telling them that they were to kill their husbands that night.

Late that night, when all of the bridegrooms were asleep, all fifty brides except for one killed their husbands. When Hypermnestra was supposed to kill her husband, she looked at him with pity, even though she did not want him. She could not plunge the dagger into his chest. As she contemplated the promise she had made to her father and sisters, she decided what she was going to do. She woke up her husband, told him about the plan that she could not go through with, and helped her new husband to flee.

When Hypermnestra's father found out about her deception, he threw her into prison for disobeying him. The other forty-nine sisters were punished by the gods for murdering their husbands. For all of eternity, these sisters are made to take jars with holes in them to a river, fill them, and carry them back, only to discover that the jars are empty and start the journey again. ❀

Scylla and Glaucus

ON A HILL near the sea, a fisherman named Glaucus was emptying his catch on the shore. The day was long, and since he was sure the fish were dead, Glaucus was flabbergasted that some of them began to revive and slip down the shore to the sea where they swam away. In his surprise, Glaucus stared at the sea in amazement, thinking that he was crazy. He scrutinized the shore where he had placed the fish, and, in doing so, wondered if the grass possessed some magic. Without thinking, Glaucus picked up a handful of grass and began to eat it.

In a matter of seconds, Glaucus was transformed. He could think of nothing other than to run and jump into the water. The impulse was uncontrollable. He ran to the sea and bounded into the waves. The gods of the sea were happy and called upon Ocean and Tethys to make Glaucus immortal. In a rushing flood of one hundred rivers, Glaucus lost consciousness. When he recuperated, he was a sea-god. His hair was green like the sea, and his body was perfect with a tail, like that of a fish. The other sea-gods thought him perfect, but to those who lived on land, Glaucus was strange and disgusting.

One day, Glaucus appeared to Scylla, a lovely nymph who was bathing in a little bay.

When Scylla saw this half-man, half-fish, she quickly fled to a point high above the strange sight, from which she could study Glaucus for a distance. Glaucus called out to the scared nymph, "Do not be frightened. I am no monster. I am a god, and I love you." Scylla was unmoved and hid from Glaucus' sight.

Glaucus was devastated because his heart was set on Scylla. In great despair, he went to Circe, the sorceress, to request a love potion that he could use on the nymph. Circe listened to Glaucus' tale, but, instead of giving Glaucus the love potion, she herself fell in love with him. Circe tried her best to win the love of Glaucus, but to no avail. He could only reply, "Time will end before I cease to love Scylla. Water will cover the world and there will be no land before I will give her up."

Upon hearing these words, Circe was furious, not at man who had rejected her, but at the nymph who was the cause of the rejection. In her anger, Circe concocted a strong, deadly poison, went to the bay where Scylla was known to bathe, and poured the poison into the water. When Scylla arrived to take her ritual bath, she turned into a terrible monster with both dog and snake heads. Scylla tried to run away, but she had been joined to the rock. In time, Scylla grew used to her fate and was happy only when she could destroy any ships that came within her reach. ❖

Pomona and Vertumnus

POMONA, A WOOD-nymph, was known for her love of the garden and cultivating fruit. She would rather spend her days pruning apple trees than caring for forests and rivers. Her passion was so great that she locked herself away from all people in order to garden undisturbed.

Pomona was pursued by a crafty young man, Vertumnus, who, try as he might, could not win her heart. Vertumnus would often disguise himself just to see her. Vertumnus was satisfied to simply catch sight of Pomona and gaze at her beautiful face, as he knew that she could never love someone like him.

One day, Vertumnus came to Pomona wearing the clothes of an old woman. She entered the garden and began to admire Pomona's fruit. Vertumnus told Pomona that the beauty of the fruit was unsurpassed. He then began kissing her, not as an old woman would have kissed a maiden, but as a young man would. Pomona was taken back by the kiss and Vertumnus took the opportunity to try to teach Pomona a lesson about a tree that was in her garden.

In the garden was an elm entwined with a vine full of ripe grapes. Vertumnus praised the tree and the vine.

"In all of its splendor, if the tree stood alone, it would not be as lovely as it is when it is with the vine, and if the vine were alone, it would not be as lovely as it is entwined in the tree. The vine would lay fruitless on the ground because it cannot stand alone."

As he spoke, Pomona watched him carefully. Vertumnus continued, "Why can you not take a lesson from the tree and the vine? Are you not the same being who turns away all who court you? Listen to me. Vertumnus loves you more than life itself, and you reject him. He loves you and only you, and, like you, he loves the land. You two could work together."

With those words, Vertumnus began to tell Pomona how much Venus despised those who were not open to love.

"This is a warning," he said. "Submit to your true love."

When he finished speaking, he removed his disguise and stood vulnerable before Pomona. Pomona was warmed by the sight of him as if the sun had burst through the clouds. ❁

Arion

ARION, A VIRTUOSO lyre player, had just won a musical competition in Sicily. He was sailing back to Corinth when he was attacked by sailors intent on stealing his prize.

"Prepare to meet your death, dear musician!" they jeered, laying hands on him. Arion begged for one last request.

"Please, allow me die as I have lived. Allow me to sing my death song, and when I have done so, I will willingly jump into the tormented sea."

The sailors agreed, as all they were really concerned with was Arion's ultimate death. They listened as Arion strummed his lyre and sang his swan song.

Arion's voice and music were carried across the waves. The song penetrated to the greatest depths of the sea, and all of its inhabitants listened intently. Creatures began to trail behind the ship as if enthralled by a magic spell. When Arion had finished, he did as he had promised and dove into the sea, only to be carried to land by the dolphins that had been listening to his glorious music. ❁

Aurora and Tithonus

AURORA, THE GODDESS of the dawn, fell in love with and married a mortal. Knowing that, unlike her, he would eventually grow old and die, Aurora approached Zeus to ask him to grant her husband immortality. Zeus agreed to, but Aurora had overlooked one important part detail in her request: she had forgotten that because Tithonus was not a god, he would continue to grow old, even though he would no longer have to die.

Days passed; soon years had, while Tithonus continued to age. His hair whitened, his limbs became weak, and he began to lose control of his mind. Aurora locked Tithonus in a chamber in her palace and left him there, not to die but to remain alone forever. In the room, Tithonus babbled incessantly; soon he could no longer move, not even to raise his head. He prayed to the gods to spare him from his misery, but there was no recourse. He was to live on forever, growing older and older.

Finally, unable to stand the constant chatter and weakened condition of her husband, Aurora turned Tithonus into a small but noisy grasshopper. ✿

Dryope

DRYOPE AND HER sister Iole strolled to the bank of a stream where they were hoping to find enough flowers to make delicate garlands for the nymphs. As they picked, Dryope clutched her first child to her chest and handed him purple lotus flowers. The child seemed to be enchanted by their brilliant color. Then Dryope noticed that blood was flowing from one of the lotus stems. To her surprise, Dryope saw that the lotus blossom was actually the nymph called Lotis, who must have transformed herself into the flower to avoid some pursuer.

Dryope stared at the blood-soaked stem, horror-stricken, and as she turned to run away, she found that she could not move: her feet were fully rooted to the ground. Helplessly, Dryope tried to tear her feet from the ground. As Iole watched in terror, Dryope was enveloped by bark. Her hair turned to leaves.

When the bark had reached Dryope's face, her husband happened to approach. He asked for his wife and Iole pointed to the newly-formed lotus. Devastated, Dryope's husband and sister embraced her warm trunk and showered it with their tears.

In her last moments, Dryope cried out to her husband and sister, "I have done no wrong. I did not intentionally hurt Lotis! If you love me, let my son play under my branches. Let no axe harm me, so that when he is older he will learn the story of his mother and mourn for her. Teach him never to pluck flowers; every bush may hold a nymph. O, do not let my son forget me! Let him come to me and call me mother!"

With those last anguished words, Dryope's lips could move no more. The bark closed over her face, and she was hidden forever. ✾

Arachne

A YOUNG PEASANT GIRL named Arachne publicly declared that her weaving was superior to anyone else's. The goddess Athena, who also wove, was outraged by the implied insult. Athena went to Arachne's hut and challenged her to a contest to determine who was the finest weaver.

The two weavers faced each other from their looms. Magnificent threads were heaped on the floor, shimmering in gold and silver. Rainbows of color were intertwined as they were woven into the finest tapestry. Athena and Arachne finished at the same moment.

Athena's work was beautiful, but Arachne's was just as magnificent. When

Athena realized that the contest would end in a draw, she tore Arachne's tapestry from top to bottom and began to beat the girl.

Arachne was confused. She knew that she had woven as well as Athena; yet, somehow, she had disgraced herself. In mortification, Arachne hanged herself.

When Athena discovered what had happened, she regretted the way she had treated Arachne. When she found Arachne's body still entangled in the noose, Athena carefully lifted her fragile corpse. Then she turned Arachne into a spider, a transformation that allowed her to continue her skillful weaving for the rest of time. ✾

Clytie and Helios

A WATER-NYMPH BY the name of Clytie was in love with Helios, the god of the sun. Helios did not return Clytie's affection, and Clytie spent her days sitting despondently, pining and turning her face upward so she could pass the day watching the rise and fall of her love. She gazed at the sun when he rose and followed his brilliance as it passed through the sky. At last, Clytie was transformed into a flower, the sunflower that forever turns toward the sun. ✾

COMPREHENSION CHECK

1. All of the myths in "The House of Athens" involve people who suffer from some misfortune. Which myth do you believe demonstrates the greatest tragedy and why?

2. Explain the story behind the voices and songs of the swallow and the nightingale.

3. In the myth of Cecrops, how do you think that Greeks reacted to a woman controlling the city rather than a man?

4. What role does Beauty play in the myths of Procne and Philomela, Scylla and Glaucus, and Pomona and Vertumnus?

5. How is Cephalus punished in the myth of Cephalus and Procris? Do you believe the punishment is justified? Why or why not?

6. Why were the people of Athens punished for not letting Boreas marry Orithyia?

7. In the myths that you have read, describe the reactions of the women as they respond to the actions of the males.

8. How do we know that the gods and goddesses made poor judges of morality?

GENERAL GOALS FOR THE CLASS

As a result of being involved in this Cooperative Learning Unit, the student will

1. more effectively learn the material as a result of having the opportunity to examine multiple points of view.

2. develop and practice those social skills that are important for learning material in class or functioning in a group at work.

3. recognize and practice those intellectual skills associated with critical reasoning as ideas are formed, examined, challenged, and elaborated on in a small group setting.

SPECIFIC OBJECTIVES FOR THIS UNIT

A. **Interaction Skills:** *As a result of the unit, the student will be able to*

1. actively participate in expressing, explaining, supporting, defending, qualifying, and elaborating on ideas in order to further the ends of the group.

2. question, praise, and encourage others in the group in order to further the ends of the group.

3. work with others to organize and present a group project.

B. **Language Arts Skills:** *As a result of the unit, the student will*

1. practice reading and writing skills.

2. expand his/her vocabulary and become aware of the origin of words that come to us from classical mythology.

3. become aware of those characters, objects, and situations from classical mythology that are important allusions and frameworks for Western culture.

4. employ those higher level cognitive skills that require the student to analyze, synthesize, evaluate, and create.

5. understand the function and role of myth in society.

SUGGESTED PROCEDURES FOR THIS UNIT

After the teacher reviews the objectives, the student roles and, if appropriate, the behavior checklist with the students, the teacher may wish to consider the following schedule. While the schedules and procedures may need to be altered in order to deal with the individual needs and abilities of each class, we offer it as a starting point.

TO THE STUDENT

Group Projects

Upon completing the readings and individual activities, each group completes one project selected from those below. At this time review the projects and discuss them, *but the group need not make its choice until the reading and individual activities are completed.* The individual activities are designed to prepare materials that may be used in the group project.

1. Publish the **Mount Olympus Herald,** a weekly newspaper which incorporates the stories, articles, cartoons, and letters that you've already written.

2. Present a panel discussion that reports on the origin and function of myth in a society.

3. Create a product (for instance, - a board game) or products (for instance, a set of posters or playing cards) that would help a student learn about classical mythology.

4. Stage a courtroom trial in which Medea (or another figure) is tried for his/her crimes.

5. Put on a talk show in which Larry King interviews individually, or in pairs, characters from the tales.

6. Taking one or more of the myths that you have dramatized by adding dialogue and stage directions, expand on that dramatization and present it to the class.

Individual and Group Activities

Day #1   In class, read Chapters 1 and 2 and write answers to the questions. If necessary, complete the assignment for homework.

Day #2   Discuss the questions in small groups and ascertain that all group members have the same understanding of the selections. Then review the list of individual activities. This should be a brainstorming session in which everyone throws out ideas and each person makes brief notes. Each member then chooses the project that he/she will work on that night.

Day #3   In the groups, individual activities are shared, critiques can be offered, and notes made for a later revision. Chapters 3 and 4 are to be read, and the comprehension questions completed for homework.

Day #4   Chapters 3 and 4 should be discussed with the object of ascertaining that everyone understands the material. After the list of individual activities is brainstormed, each group member selects the project he/she will complete that evening.

Day #5   In groups, share individual activities, critique, and revise as necessary. Chapters 5 and 6 are to be completed for homework.

Day #6   Discuss Chapters 5, 6, and 7, and brainstorm a list of individual activities; each group member again choosing the individual activity he/she will complete.

Day #7   After sharing, critiquing, and revising individual activities, choose what will be the group project and begin work on it. Students may need to make revisions to some materials at home.

Days #8, 9, 10 Work in groups organizing and completing the group projects. (To complete the task within this time framework, students may need to do some of the work at home.)

Days #11 & #12 Present to the class your group's project.

Individual Activities

- This program requires each student to read each chapter, answer the comprehension questions, and complete the individual activity he or she has chosen. The activity the students choose does not have to be the same activity that others in the group pick.

- As a newspaper journalist, meet a returning hero or heroine and write a newspaper article about his or her adventures.

- As a talk show host, invite two or more of the figures in the book to your show. Write the dialogue that takes place between these people and/or gods and goddesses.

- Create a scenario for a courtroom-based drama. Identify the characters, conflicts, charges, and countercharges.

- Do research on the origin and functions of myths and write a report based on your findings. Be sure to read Edith Hamilton's introduction to her book, *Mythology, Timeless Tales of Gods and Heroes*.

- From the narrative in your book, choose an incident or incidents and dramatize it/them by writing stage directions and dialogue for the characters.

- Write a scenario for a movie in which you retell the basic story, but place your characters and actions in modern times.

- Come up with a concept for a board game that involves the myth and mythological characters in the chapter you have just read. State the general design and objective of the game and list some of the rules.

- Conduct an interview in Hades with two of the characters in the chapter.

- Meet with a mythological character and a more modern counterpart from fiction, for example Thisbe and Juliet. With you as a host for a PBS television program, write some questions you would ask and answers that the guests give.

- In the style of a tabloid journalist, write a news article on an incident or incidents that supposedly "really" happened.

- Draw a three or four-panel comic strip that is based on mythology. Use bubbles to show dialogue. Invent a catchy title for your strip.

- Create a map for one myth.

- Write an editorial for a newspaper in which you attack or defend the actions of one of the heroes, gods, or goddesses.

- Compare or contrast Hercules to someone you feel is a modern hero.

- Create a wall chart depicting god and goddesses, myhtological heroes, deeds, or families.

- Compare creation myths from different cultures.*

*See Leeming's *The World of Myth* or Eliot's *The Universal Myths*, both available from Prestwick House.

Who's Who

Roman Name	Greek Name	Parents	Symbol	Identity
	Achilles	King Peleus and Thetis (nymph)		Hero of the Greek camp in the Trojan War. Invulnerable except for a weak spot on his heel – his "Achilles heel."
	Acrisius			King of Argos. Father to Danae. Grandfather to Perseus.
	Aegisthus	Pelopea and Thyestes		Adulterous lover of Clytemnestra while Agamemnon was away at Troy. Killer of Agamemnon, killed by Agamemnon's son, Orestes
Aeneas		Anchises and Aphrodite (Venus)		A hero of Troy. Founder of Rome.
	Agamemnon	Aerope and Atreus		Commander of the Greek forces at Troy. Husband of Clytemnestra. Father to Iphigenia.
	Andromeda	Cepheus and Cassiopeia		Became Perseus' wife. Great-grand-mother of Hercules.
	Antigone	Jocasta and Oedipus		Faced death when she disobeyed her uncle Creon's edict not to bury her brother Polyneices.
Venus	Aphrodite	Dione and Zeus	Dove	Goddes of Love
Arachne			Spider	Changed into a spider by Minerva (Athena) after challenging the goddess to a weaving contest.
Mars	Ares	Hera and Zeus	Vulture	God of War
	Argonauts			Journeyed with Jason on the Quest of the Golden Fleece
	Ariadne	Pasiphae and Minos (of Crete)		Lover of Theseus, helped him discover a way out of the labyrinth.
Diana	Artemis	Leto and Zeus	Cypress and Deer	Goddess of the Hunt, and (as Apollo's twin sister) of the Moon
	Augeas			King of Elis, owner of thousands of cattle in a filthy stable. Hercules had to clean out the stables as his fifth labor.
Aurora	Eos	Theia and Hyperion (Titans)		Goddess of the Dawn
Baucis				Wife of Philemon who, with her husband, offered hospitality to Jupiter and Mercury.
Bacchus	Dionysus	Semele and Zeus		God of wine and joy
	Theseus	Aethra and Aegeus		King of Athens. Hero of many adventures, especially killing the Minotaur and escaping the labyrinth.

Roman Name	Greek Name	Parents	Symbol	Identity
Aquilo	Boreas	Eos and Astraeus		The North Wind.
	Cecrops	Erechtheus (King of Athens)		Great-grandfather of Theseus.
	Charon	Nyx (Night) and Erebus (primordial darkness)		Aged man who ferried the souls of the dead across the river Acheron to the gates of the Underworld.
	Charybdis	Gaia and Poseidon		Whirlpool in the Strait of Messina opposite the rocky cave where the sea monster Scylla lives.
	Circe	Perse and Helios		Witch who turned Odysseue's men into swine.
	Clytemnestra	Leda and Tyndareus		Wife and murderer of Agamemnon. Mother to Iphigenia and Orestes
	Clytie			Mortal turned into a sunflower because of her unrequited love for Apollo.
	Creusa	Erechtheus (King of Athens)		Mother to Ion.
	Cyclops	Mother Earth (Gaea) and Father Heaven (Ouranos)		Race of powerful giants with a single eye in the middle of their foreheads.
	Daedalus	Metion		Grandson to Erechthius, King of Athens. Builder of the labrynth of Crete. Imprisoned by King Minos, escapes by crafting wings frong birds' feathers and wax.
	Danaids	Danaus, a descendent of Io		Forty-nine sisters who slew their husbands on their wedding nights. As punishment, each travels continuously to the river to fill a water jar riddled with holes.
	Diomedes	Tydeus and Deipyle		King of Thrace who owned a herd of man-eating horses. Fought for Greece in the Trojan War. Later slain by Hercules.
	Dryope	Eurytus		Transformed into a Lotus tree by the nymph Lotis for plucking blossons from a Lotus tree.
	Eetes	Perse and Helios		King of Colchis, "owner" of the Golden Fleece. Father to Medea.
	Eurystheus	Sthenelus		King of Mycene. Cousin to Hercules. Devised the Twelve Labors as penance for Hercules' killing of his wife and sons.

Roman Name	Greek Name	Parents	Symbol	Identity
	Epimetheus	Iapetus		Brother to Atlas (Titan) and Prometheus (Titan). Husband to Pandora.
	Glaucus			A fisherman turned to merman-sea god. Fell in love with Scylla and was indirectly the cause of Scylla's transformation into a sea monster.
Pluto	Hades	Rhea and Cronus (Titans)		King of the Dead; god of the underworld.
Sol	Helios	Theia and Hyperion (Titans)	Whip and Globe	The Sun God.
Vulcan	Hephaestus	Hera and Zeus		God of Fire. Blacksmith of the gods.
Mercury	Hermes	Maia and Zeus		Messenger and herald of the gods.
	Icarus	Daedalus		Flew too close to the sun (escaping from Crete with his father), and plunged in the sea.
	Io	Inachus		Turned into a heifer by Zeus to hide his infidelity. Sentence to remain a heifer and wander the earth forever by a jealous Hera.
	Iphigenia	Clytemnestra and Agamemnon		Sacrificed by Agamemnon on his way to the Trojan War.
	Medea	Etes, King of Colchis		Granddaughter of Helios, first wife to Jason. Used sorcery and murder for her own ends. Killed: her brother, her sons, Pelias, and Jason's second wife (and wife's father Creon). Attempted to kill Theseus while married to Theseus' father.
	Narcissus	Liriope (nymph) and Cephissus (river god)		Beautiful youth who fell in love with own reflection and died. The flower, narcissus, sprang up where the youth died.
	Oedipus	Jocasta and Laius		King of Thebes who, as prophesied by the Oracle at Delphi, murdered his father and married his mother.
	Orestes	Clytemnestra and Agamemnon		Avenges his father's murder at the hands of his mother and her lover.
	Orithyia	Erechtheus (King of Athens)		Sister to Procris. Wife to Boreas.
	Pelias	Tyro and Poseidon		Sent Jason on his quest for the Golden Fleece in order to circumvent a prophesy that Jason would be the cause of Pelias's downfall.

Roman Name	Greek Name	Parents	Symbol	Identity
	Perseus	Danae and Zeus		Greek hero of many adventures including slaying a Medusa. Husband to Andromeda. Great-grandfather to Hercules.
	Philomela	King Pandion I of Athens		Tongue cut out by brother-in-law (Tereus, son of Ares). Wove tapestry to reveal crime. Turned into a nightingale.
Philemon				Husband to Baucis. Blessed by Jupiter and Mercury for hospitality even in the midst of poverty.
	Phineus	Agenor		King of Thrace and prophet. Blinded by Zeus and tormented by Harpies because of insightful accuracy of his prophecies.
Pomona			Pruning knife	Goddess presiding over fruit trees.
	Procne	King Pandion I of Athens		Sister to Philomela. Wife to Tereus, son of Ares. Turned into a swallow.
	Procris	Erechtheus (King of Athens)		Wife to Cephalus. Jealously spied on Cephalus while he was hunting and was accidentally killed.
	Procrustes			Legendary robber who killed his prey on his infamous bed. Finally killed by Theseus.
	Prometheus	Iapetus (Titan)		Brother to Atlas and Epimetheus (Titans). Called the "Savior of Mankind" but hated by Olympian gods for stealing fire from the gods and giving to humans for protection.
Proserpine	Persephone	Demeter (Ceres)		Maiden of the spring. Queen of the Dead (wife to Hades/Pluto)
	Psyche			Personification of the Human Soul. Wife of Eros (Cupid), was not allowed to know the identity of her husband.
Pygmalion				Misogynist sculptor who fell in love with his own sculpture – a beautiful woman he named Galatea.
Pyramus				Misogynist sculptor who fell in love with his own sculpture – a beautiful woman he named Galatea.
	Scylla			Beautiful nymph turned into a hideous sea monster by a jealous Circe.
Thisbe				Lover of Pyramus in a star-crossed story that was a source for Shakespeare's *Romeo and Juliet*.
	Tiresias	Chariclo (nymph) and Everes		Blind prophet, the most famous of all Greek seers.
	Zephyr			The West Wind
Jupiter	Zeus	Rhea and Cronus (Titans)	Eagle, lightning bolt	King of the Olympian Gods